Memories O' Mine

Growing Up in Scotland 1930 - 1954

Anna Clark Hender

MEMORIES O' MINE

GROWING UP IN SCOTLAND

1930 - 1954

by ANNA CLARK HENDER

Dedicated to my darling daughter

Heather

Cover: Bluebells are a symbol of Scotland.
Tartan is the Clark tartan.
Front cover photo is the author's family, 1946.

THE BEGINNING

1

1930 was a good year. It was the year that I was born. Not that I knew too much about it. I subsequently knew it was during the great depression years and that I had been born to a Mom and Dad in their early twenties. Both came from families of seven and eight kids so I had a large extended family. True Scots who had always lived in the land of my birth. We belonged to the Clark family (my father), I later learned that they were part of the clergy of the clans in the history of the proud Scottish heritage of mine. But at that time it little mattered, I had just entered a strange yet familiar new world.

My home town of Dundee is a seaport on the east coast of Scotland at the mouth of the river Tay where it meets the North Sea. It became a royal burgh in 1190. Here lies an interesting story. David, Earl of Huntingdon, brother of King William (The Lionhearted) had joined the Third Crusade to the Holyland. On his return journey home to England his ship was overtaken by a raging storm in the North Sea. David prayed to heaven for deliverance and, as the storm abated, vowed to build a church in gratitude to honor the Virgin Mary. From the North Sea he found safe waters at the mouth of the River Tay. Landing on the north bank he called the place Donom Dei (Gift of God). That name became Dundee. Keeping his promise he built "Saint Mary's", which to this day still stands in the center of town. In 1190, David's brother, King William granted the city it's first royal charter as a burgh. The Virgin Mary became the titular saint of the town and the pot of lilies (her emblem) was incorporated in the town's coat of arms. David, Earl of Huntington, is portrayed as Crusader Knight in a stained glass window of the church.

The year I was born Dundee was a town of approximately 142,000 people, and was known as a "jute" town which meant that most of it's business was the processing and the manufacturing of jute for ropes, burlap and sacks etc. Practically all the working folks made their living in one of the five or six jute mills in town. My Mom and Dad were no exception.

By the end of the 19th century the jute trade was flourishing and most of the work in Dundee was in the jute mills. Dundee was at the estuary of the River Tay where it empties into the North Sea which allowed for raw jute to be imported from India. A new process, using whale oil, allowed the jute to be processed by machine.

Dundee had a large whaling industry, mostly to supply the jute mills and also was a shipbuilding center, building about 200 ships a year, mostly for whaling.

Royal Geographical Society commissioned Dundee Shipbuilders Company to build a special research ship for work in Antarctic waters. So began the British National Antarctic Expedition (1901-1904) led by Robert Falcon Scott. RRS Discovery was launched from Dundee in 1901. Dundee is now known (2012) as "the city of Discovery" with the research ship RRS Discovery berthed in it's home base as a nautical museum.

I did find out that my father had a lovely tenor voice and could sure sing a song. He had the opportunity to become a chorus member in London, England, in one of the new musicals of the time. However, he was a young man in love and feared that the time away would embolden the many suitors my mother had and would not take the chance. He had met Mom in the jute mill and that was good enough for him.

I don't remember my early years. I know I was loved by my parents and extended family. When I was about two years old we moved to a two room coldwater flat. Gran and Grandpa Spiers, (mom's parents) lived downstairs in the two story building and we shared a toilet on the landing with them and my uncles and cousins. My sister Betty was born when I was two, Margaret when I was four and brother David when I was nine.

We four kids shared the one bedroom and Mom and Dad had their bed in the alcove in the kitchen. You could say we were a close family but we were no different from our friends and their families. My sisters and I shared a double brass bed, this is not as bad as it would seem, in a room with no heat we kept each other warm. Downstairs lived my Gran and Grandpa, four uncles and five cousins. My youngest uncle, in his teens, was the baby of Gran's family, he and my older uncle Bob were both single. Two other uncles one with two young children, and another with three lived with gran, I didn't know, but I guess they were there from the time they were babies. Gran was mother to them all. We never knew whether the uncles were divorced or if their wives had died. Thinking of it now I suspect it was the latter as divorce was unheard of in working folks of the twenties and thirties. But adult matters were never discussed with children and we just accepted things as they were.

THE BERRIES

2

Mom and Dad both worked and my earliest memories were of being wrapped in a blanket, against the cold damp Scottish mornings, to be sat in front of Gran's big fireplace. The fire was always burning brightly as it was the only heat in the house. The adults had already had breakfast and were on their way to work. The big kitchen was plenty busy though as Gran also cared for five of my cousins.

I don't know when Gran got time to sleep, she always had so much to do. Gran was about five foot nothing and skinny as a rail, she had so much energy and her hair was black as a raven's wing up until the day she died. I never saw Gran tired I guess she was too busy. She did have her own way of getting time to herself though as we got older. After age five we kids were in school during most of the day.

Summer was more of a problem when we had seven weeks vacation from school, but Gran had a few tricks for us. One day she would say "I hear they are starting kids at the berries today without grown-ups". This was a chance to earn a few pennies for candy. I say a few pennies because when we picked with our parents we usually ate more than we turned in. There was much excitement as five cousins, my sister and I looked forward to candy money. My sister, Margaret, and my brother were too little to go with us. We each got a bread roll in case we got hungry, (typical kids, we were always hungry).......nothing on the roll, just a bread roll and off we went. It was a little over a mile walk to the tram, that took a good hour, stopping some time looking in the candy store window to decide what we should buy with our yet-to-be-earned "berry" money. Then the tram journey took another half hour to reach the edge of town. The berry fields were now a mile away which meant another hour or more as we stopped to throw stones in the stream or watch sheep in the field.

Eventually, we were at "the berries", we marched up to the gaffer. He looked at our raggle-taggle bunch and said "Where are your folks"? On hearing that there was just us he said "no bairns without their folks to mind them". We were so disappointed but, being kids, that didn't last for long. We sneaked into the raspberry bushes. I know that our sneaking was well watched but I'm sure the gaffer once had a granny as sneaky as ours and he understood. We picked a few berries each, squished them on our rolls......that and water cupped in our hands from a nearby stream and we were one happy bunch.

Counting the return journey gran had about five hours free of us kids. She was so surprised that we weren't allowed to berry pick.

One morning a couple of weeks later gran would say "I hear they are starting kids at the berries today without grown -ups" AND IT WOULD START AGAIN. Over the summer gran could count on three days of quiet with her ploy and we kids never doubted her. After all, it was gran who always told us to never tell a lie so surely everything she told us was the truth.

EARLY SCHOOL YEARS

3

School started at five years old. No gradual introductions, from 9 in the morning 'til three in the afternoon, with one hour for lunch and two playtimes of 15 minutes each. First grade was further broken up by a couple of ten minute snack breaks. That, and a huge jar of colored candy fish on teacher's desk, handed out sparingly for a job well done, was the only concession to our age and newness. We started right away to learn the alphabet and the two times table by rote.

Our desks were single and wooden, with the seat attached, a slight sloping lid that opened to hold our one and only book (children's primer) and pencils. There was an ink well in a recess on the top part, which was like a little shelf. No ink as we did not learn to use pen and ink 'til the second grade. There were no crayons or finger paints (I don't think there was such a thing then) and no little cozy corner like in today's kindergarten. School in the thirties was a serious business.

We sat two side by side in a row facing the front with a path down the middle of the room and had maybe twenty kids to a class (boys and girls) although we were separated at playtime (recess) into two different areas with railing between. The boy's playground was always full of noise and action. The girls were quieter and played jump rope or catch-ball or just talked, in an orderly way, while chaos ruled with the boys. Although in sight of each other we completely ignored the other side.

All our teachers in grade school were women, all unmarried, teaching was not a job but a vocation. It was also an honored profession and teachers were much respected in the community.

I think that there were only two males associated with our school. The janitor, who lived in a little house on the school grounds, with his wife and four kids. And our Head Master (Principal) who was the final authority on all things in the universe to our young minds.

Grade school was from five to twelve years old. No frills, very strict, core studies and a good Scottish education. The system split at age twelve. Most students went to two years of high school where the boys were taught the beginnings of a trade, which they could continue after leaving school as an apprentice to a business. Girls were taught an office skill, plus home studies.... cooking, sewing, etc. All high school students graduated at age fourteen. The other alternative was the academies, four years of study and then you could enter the University. There was no other way to a higher education.

Being a Catholic school, we were right next to our priests' house, which was right next to the church - St Peter and Paul - which was also the name of our school.

We had catechism at the start of every school day and as we approached seven, we prepared for our first communion. One of our three priests would drop by catechism class, eventually we were quizzed on the tenets of our faith and finally the big day came. We went to confession on Friday in one of those big dark boxes with a priest on one side of a separating grilled window. The darkness was to ensure our anonymity.

What on earth did a seven year old, little, shy, obedient girl have in the way of sin in the 1930s? I confess that I made up sins so as not to disappoint the priest. I hit my little sister..... NO WAY, I said a swear word..... NO WAY, I told a lie..... thinking back on it, that was the only truth in my confession as I was lying to the priest. I was given the appropriate penance. That over with, I was ready for my First Communion.

My parents were so proud and I felt so pretty. I'm not sure what the boys wore, a dark suit I guess. The girls wore knee length white dresses, most were satin, with a little white veil, we carried little white rosaries and a shiny white covered prayer book. We walked to the school to be handed over to our teachers and then marched two by two to the church where we sat as a group in the front.

Catholic Mass in the thirties was all conducted in Latin. We never knew exactly what was said but we stood, kneeled or sat at the appropriate times. It was solemn and scary to walk up to the altar, kneel, and take my First Communion. As the priest placed the wafer on my tongue he bent down and whispered in my ear the name of my personal patron saint "Saint Theresa of the little flower". I guess my childish mind was most impressed by "the little flower".

One memory - ours being a Catholic school -our classroom had a lovely statue of the Virgin Mary in a little grotto by the window. With her soft smile and graceful blue gown she always seemed to me to bring calm to the room.

In ancient Roman culture, the month of May (the official Spring) signified new life and fertility and the Motherhood of Mother Earth. In the late eighteen hundreds the Catholic church dedicated the month of May to Mary the Mother of Jesus. Our classroom bloomed with colour and fragrance at this time as there was a garden of beauty around Mary's statue. Many in our classroom had family who grew flowers in their allotments so flowers were plentiful and free. As we sang at the beginning of class.

BRING FLOWERS OF THE RAREST
BRING BLOSSOMS THE FAIREST
FROM GARDEN AND WOODLAND
AND HILLSIDE AND VALE
OUR FULL HEARTS ARE SWELLING
OUR GLAD VOICES TELLING
THE PRAISE OF THE LOVELIEST
FLOWER OF THE VALE.

O MARY! WE CROWN THEE WITH BLOSSOMS TODAY
QUEEN OF THE ANGELS AND QUEEN OF THE MAY
O MARY! WE CROWN THEE WITH BLOSSOMS TODAY
QUEEN OF THE ANGELS AND QUEEN OF THE MAY.

This memory I will always cherish. In the mind of my childhood it was a small measure of a time set aside, full of beauty, peace and love.

School was quite uneventful, I was good at my studies... sat in the back of the class with the "smart" kids and progressed thru' the grades without any trouble (in those days, if you failed your final exam you were held back in the grade for another year - a great incentive to do well).

I was not punished too many times during my school years, remember that I was shy and quiet and obedient, but I remember one Spring day when my best friend and I had a giggling fit. Every time we looked at each other we started to giggle. You would think we would stop looking at each other but we just could not.....giggle, giggle, giggle. Voice of authority "Anna and Cathy come here at once. What are you giggling about?" "Don't know" we said. Then we looked at each other and started giggling again..... Out came the leather strap from teacher's desk. "hold out your hand"..... two straps each... boy, did they sting, and our hands were red......but we sure stopped giggling.

When I was eleven my last year in grade school, my teacher entered me into a competition for the Leng Silver Medal. This singing competition was held every year in the Dundee schools. Sir John Leng, owner of our newspaper and member of Parliament for Dundee set up the Leng Trust to promote and encourage the teaching of the songs of Scotland. This trust started in 1901 and still is in effect today. A silver medal for singing was awarded once yearly to each public school. Silver medalists thru' age sixteen competed each year for the Gold Medal. A coveted prize in our school system.

our song was chosen from a list of Scottish Folk Songs (four in all) designated by the judges. Teacher would assign the class some reading while she worked with the competitors.

One afternoon we were told that the competitors for the Leng Medal were to go to the gymnasium. Thinking it was for some announcement we all trooped in, only to find an accompanist at the piano and three judges waiting for us. SURPRISE!!! (these were the war years and things were not done in the usual manner). After our singing and the judges conferring, my name was called. I had become a Leng Silver Medalist. Medal and award ceremony to be at a school assembly at a later date.

We all trooped back to our respective class rooms. Upon entering my class it was the last part of the afternoon and we were doing "poetry". This was so dull and boring as the whole class, as one, recited poetry of our teacher's choosing. We recited it by rote just like we did the two times two table....IT WAS AWFUL. I sat down and joined the others.

After school I told some of my classmates in the hallway that I had won the medal. "You had better go back and tell teacher or she will be mad" said my friend Cathy.....Back to the classroom, told teacher, she said "good girl" and patted me on the head.

Back in the hallway my classmates wanted to know what teacher said "she was pleased" I said. One boy in the group put everything in perspective. In a surly and accusatory voice he loudly said "You should have told her when you came in and we could have gotten out of poetry"

WASH DAY

4

Out back of the flats (the backies) was a wash house and two drying greens. The greens were surrounded by wooden picket fences. There was grass underfoot and clothes lines overhead.

A row of cellars, each about the size of a large hall closet was on one side of the greens. These were storage sheds for all of us renters. As we had nothing for storage our shed made great "club house" for us kids. As there were five cousins plus me and my siblings it was a tight squeeze but there was something exciting about sitting on an old carpet that Gran had given us. In the dark, musty space, with only a dim flashlight for light there was no "club" business or discussion. We mostly sat around and told ghost stories and scared ourselves silly.

Each family was assigned a specific wash day. It was not a favorite day for us kids....we had work to do and had to fend for ourselves when it came to meals - usually meat pies from the bakery, as Mum spent the best part of the day doing the week's worth of washing for our family.

The wash house was a large square room with a boiler on one side and three deep sinks on the other with a hand cranked clothes wringer between them. Two small windows over the sinks gave the only light. Mum stood on a small wooden platform, about three inches from the floor. This was more comfortable than standing on the COLD concrete . The ritual on wash day was always the same. Before going to work in the Jute Mill Dad would start the fire under the boiler and ladle pots of water from the cold water tap over the sink in the opposite corner. By the time Mum was ready, the boiler water was bubbling and the room was filled with steam. The wash house building was made of concrete blocks so, even with the fire and steam and boiling water, it was still a cold and draughty place.

When we were five years old we had to contribute, our job was to lug the clothes basket down one flight of stairs and out to the wash house, making about three or four trips for our family. Of the three sinks one held water and a detergent, (I think it was called Persil)one had "blue" water, (some substance used to whiten the clothes) and one clear cold water for rinsing.

The clothes were first scrubbed on a wash board in the "Persil" sink, using some of the hot water from the boiler as we had only cold water taps. These clothes were then plopped into the boiler which by now was steaming and boiled for about twenty minutes while Mum scrubbed more clothes on the corrugated wash board in the sink. The steaming clothes from the boiler were the caught on the end of a long stout stick and slung over to the "blue" water sink to be whitened and brightened. We kids had to stay out during the slinging process as we could have gotten a bad burn if we came in contact with the boiling clothes. From the "blueing" water to the rinsing water(or was it the other way around?) then thru' the hand cranked wringer attached to one of the sinks.This was the first batch done. This process was to continue for hours.

As we got older we kids had to lug the finished batches out to the drying green and, using wooden pegs, hang the clothes out to dry. This was somewhat feasible in the summer, despite the Scottish rain, but I have memories of Mum washing the clothes in the semi-light of a winter's day. This was done by candle-light as there was no electricity and how she got them dried I'm blessed if I know. I remember if it wasn't raining or snowing Mum would hang the wash out a few at a time. When they were sufficiently frozen and stiff as a board (Mum said they always smelled better for the fresh air)she would transfer them to a wooden rack on a pulley in the kitchen, so that the heat from the cooking and the fire would dry them as they hung over our heads. David's nappies (diapers) could not wait for the pulley when he was a baby so his diapers were hung on trivets by the fire. Rain or snow, you only had one day to use the wash house and you made the best of it. If the weather was too bad, it was quite simple, the wash was not done, and we had no fresh clothes for that week.

Did I say that wash day was not my favorite day? As a child I didn't appreciate that it was a more unfavorite day for Mum. No one complained, the wash was just something that had to be done. There was also quite a bit of pride involved in having a "good wash" with sparkling whites and bright colors. After all, the whole neighborhood just had to look out their windows to see... and there was much gossip about the merits of anyone who hung out a dingy wash.

CAMPING

5

Just a few weeks before the summer holidays.....it has started. We kids were excited enough about school being out...then we would notice the luxuries being hoarded. Chocolate biscuits, tinned ham, tinned peaches, tinned treacle and syrup. Not the kind that we filled from the barrel at the store. We usually liked to see Mum get her syrup and treacle this way as it looked so gooey as it oozed from the barrel. But anything tinned was really living and.....WE KNEW. We were going on our annual holiday to Barry Camp.

Packing our clothes was no problem (we didn't have many) nobody cared what you wore or how clean you were when living in a tent. There was a communal water spot at one end of the camp. A few cold water taps for all water needs. Drinking, cooking, washing (dishes and people)...no showers, after all this was camp in the thirties. Great that Mum was not too observant of our cleanliness. After all, this was camp and she was on holiday as well.

Barry was about forty miles from my home town of Dundee, midway between Monifieth and Carnoustie. Dad walked about a three mile round trip early each morning to Monifieth Bakery for our breakfast rolls. Life was good, though to us kids life was just life. But when I think of cold summer mornings, everything sparkling and smelling good after the usual Scottish rain, strong tea with plenty of sugar and milk, fresh rolls with butter or jam and a whole day ahead with nothing but play and running a few errands, could life be any better than this? We kids were so happy and carefree.

Don't remember much about setting up camp. I guess Mum and Dad would rather that we weren't in the way. I was about seven years old at the time Betty was five and Margaret was three. I remember that mattress bags were filled with straw as were the pillows. I loved how everything crackled as we bedded down.

It must have been a power of work to set up camp but we kids were oblivious to that fact. We were sent to the camp store for essentials, if we were having a good day we got candies (sweeties) for the family, a rare treat but it was the holidays. Betty and I also had the job of carrying water for cooking purposes.

Our tent was quite a way from the water spot which was always quite noisy and it took us a couple trips and a long time to get this job done. I now suspect that Dad replenished the water when we were out playing or waving at the trains. We didn't notice and were secure in the fact that we did a great job as water carriers. Mum sometimes mentioned how good the tea tasted, "it must be because you carried the water so carefully".

We went to the farm next door for milk or eggs. Milk was still warm from the morning milking. One morning, looking for adventure, Betty and I decided that, instead of the path, we would take a shortcut through the field. Climbing over the fence, little hearts pounding like mad, we ran as fast as we could to get to the farmhouse, sure that the HUGE cows (all two of them) were racing after two little girls to have them for breakfast. If we had been able to look back we would have seen them leisurely chewing the grass and possibly wondering what all the fuss was about.

We renewed our play with kids from other towns nearby who also came to Barry every year. A railroad went by the camp and we waited for the passenger trains so that we could wave to all the people. While waiting for the trains we spent much time hunting for bugs. We would lie in the tall grass, watch the clouds and count how many different shapes we could see. Next to the railroad was the Carnoustie Golf Links and a nearby Army Camp. We would take the path through the Links and then through the Army Camp to get to the beach.

Running around, playing, and doing nothing in the country/ocean air was tiring and we were not too upset when we had our tea and biscuits and were off to bed. As we were drifting off to sleep we could hear "Taps" being played at the Army Camp. It sounded so lonely yet so calm and secure. Always same time, same tune and sounded so peaceful. I found out later the words used for taps "Day is done, Gone the sun, from the hills, from the lake, from the skies. All is well, safely rest. God is nigh". The words fit the peacefulness of the music.

Night-time was now for the grown-ups. With all the kids safely in their tents, presumably asleep, our parents would gather around the campfire, relax and talk. Someone always brought his accordion and the singing would start.... Falling asleep, smell of the wood fire, people singing, snug in bed in our tent, I felt so loved and secure.

After two weeks we said "cheerio" to our friends and took the bus back to town where, it still being the summer holidays, we played, did nothing, and ran errands, but it wasn't the same.

There were not too many more years at Barry Camp..... World War 2 started in the Autumn of 1939. The quiet, peaceful years were over and such turmoil and hurt about to begin. I was nine years old at the time and fifteen when the war finally ended.

GRANDPA'S GARDEN

6

They are called "The Allotments" but Grandpa had a garden in every sense of the word. It was a little over a mile from their home (a cold water flat) and about ten to twelve minutes walk away. He paid Feu Duty on the land to the city council. It was just a pittance or working folk could not afford it. Living in crowded flats in town there was no way to have a garden or grow some food, and the allotments afforded working people the chance to do just that. The allotments are still in use and rent is paid to the city for the land. Feu Duty could be traced to feudalism, when serfs worked the master's land and received a small plot of land for themselves to grow what they needed.

The main purpose of Grandpa's Garden was to supply vegetables for the family but it also fed our need for beauty. As children we did not appreciate but just absorbed the garden in it's entirety.

Located on Law Hill, the highest point in our city and just beyond the gray tenements of town, the trees and grass made it seem like the countryside. There was a little "greenhouse" which was needed for growing tomatoes and some special flowers. These were grown under glass as the Scottish weather was not conducive to growing them outdoors. Back to Grandpa's house made of glass. You entered into a small separate room which had a small fireplace for heat. A little additional heat for the tomatoes and flowers and to keep Granpa comfortable in the cool Scottish weather. At a built-in sort of desk Grandpa kept all his seed catalogues. High point of the year was when the new catalogues were delivered........ he and his friend from the allotment next door would pore over these in the late autumn and winter months and map out their growing plans for the coming year.

Picture the scene...in the cold, dreary Scottish winter months, the world is gray and the rain pouring down... two old gentlemen, after a lifetime of work and raising families now have time to spare....there they are in the little front room of the greenhouse, just a couple of chairs, a large old desk, and a small fire to keep them warm. And on the desk, seed catalogues...... spread in front of them next year's flowers and veggies..... you can see the colors, smell the flowers and taste the vegetables as they dream of how their gardens will be. All from teeny, tiny seeds, there are miracles all around when you are a gardener.

I don't know if Grandpa started his garden when a young man with a family to feed or if he started after he retired. I know he was a "half-timer" in the Jute mill, starting at age twelve, half a day at school and half in the mill. At fourteen school was finished, and the mill was full time. Not many years of education, but a good Scottish education, Grandpa's love of learning lasted him a lifetime. He knew all the flowers and veggies by their horticultural names.

Come with me as I remember. There was a high wooden fence around the entrance of the allotments and a few steps up to the earthen path round the rentals, Grandpa was first up from the street. There was a four foot picket fence on three sides and a chinked stone wall at the back, separating him from another series of plots. Stone wall was about eight feet high. As you entered the garden the greenhouse was to the right, with a wooden bench in front which also stored gardening tools.

In front of this, to the left was a flower garden with daffodils, tulips, asters and iris in their season. Going up the path towards the stone wall, to the right there was a bed with sloping glass covers where Grandpa germinated the seeds. Further up was a high string framework which supported sweet peas, runners full of beautiful, delicate colors and perfume. Beyond that was a patch of cabbage and Brussels sprouts. The path thru' the middle of the garden was lined with little dwarf bushes, behind these were pansies of every color. Half-way up the path was a wooden arch trellis ablaze with rambler roses. Path ended at the wall with a seat and a trellis covered with more roses.

Growing along the wall were wallflowers, rich colors that looked like velvet. Path went by the wall to the compost heap, which was at the furthest corner..across the path was planted rhubarb (for Granma's yummy pies and to use with custard). From back to front of this area were, beets, carrots, lettuce, green peas and potatoes. These were all grown in their season, when one crop was finished another was planted in the soil. For a small plot of land every inch was put to good use. Yes, Grandpa was quite a gardener, of course, many men of his generation were excellent gardeners out of necessity. The entire extended family always had fresh flowers and vegetables for our homes.

One special thing was the Chrysanthemums grown in the greenhouse, they were pure white, huge blooms with curled petals. People would come to the allotments on Sunday to buy flowers for the cemetery. In November was a special remembrance day... a tradition. And the beautiful white blooms were sold at a pittance for this purpose..... Grandpa lost money on these flowers but they were a gift of love and respect to people who were honoring their loved ones.

On the morning of May 3rd, my twenty-first birthday, I remember answering the door to find Grandma and Grandpa on the front steps with two wicker baskets................. they had picked EVERY DAFFODIL in his garden to honor my special day. Remember that these were among the first flowers of Spring in Scotland and the first money that Grandpa would make that year....WHAT A GESTURE OF LOVE.....the house was filled with Spring and the brightness of the sun in the yellow flowers made me forget the gray dreariness of the Scottish weather.

DAVID

7

The month after my ninth birthday, something real special happened. Mum went into the hospital..... much excitement, we girls were told that we now had a baby brother and he was to be called David, after our father. Mum was in hospital for three weeks and we surely missed her, but a baby all of our own to play with was going to be a great adventure, and we were old enough to help. I was nine, Betty seven and Margaret five.

As David was born in June, there was no school and no homework to do. With Gran and Granpa downstairs, along with the uncles and cousins, we didn't lack for company while Dad was at work. And both of our grandmas made sure we were well fed. Grandma Clark would take us every other day to the hospital where we could see Mum and she could see us.

Children were not allowed in the hospital, so we stood in the park outside. Mum was on the first floor and we held a yelling conversation for a few minutes with her at the open window. It was a short time but we knew Mum was all right.

After three weeks in the hospital mum was coming home with our new baby.

Standing at the street corner looking for the taxi bringing Mum, Dad, and baby home was a day I won't forget. After spotting the car, we ran after it all the way up the lane so we could at last see our baby brother.

Everything was ready, the big laundry basket in the corner had been turned into a cozy nest for the wee one. The high sides kept out the Scottish drafts and it had two handles for carrying. Baby had to adapt to the noise and cuddling of a large family as all came to see our baby. Thirteen siblings of my parents, who had all married, and had two or three kids each. That and two sets of grandparents plus our own family, we were quite a clan.

They all helped take care of us in our little But and Ben (room and kitchen). Crowded? We didn't know the meaning of the word... we were just us and all this was normal.

Baby was just three weeks old when he was christened at our Catholic church. This was a special occasion and the whole family came to Gran's house to celebrate. Gran had more space than we had and she lived just downstairs from our two rooms.

Although a name had been chosen... by Scottish tradition a baby was not called by his or her name until the name was given by the priest at the Christening Ceremony.

Everyone gathered at Gran's and when all were there the Christening Party set out for the church. In the Roman Catholic Church a christening was not done during services but was a small private ceremony held in a closed off room in the back of the church which had a christening font as the only furniture.

The Christening Party, by tradition, consisted of the two parents and the Godparent who carried the baby. This Godparent had to be an unmarried young woman. As a nineteen year old I had the honor of being Godparent to my Uncle Harry's new baby.

At the appointed hour the party stood by the font and waited for the priest to arrive. After checking on the family, making sure they were parishioners of the church, and also the name to be given there was a short ceremony during which holy water was poured from the font onto the head of the baby as the priest intoned, "I christen thee David in the name of The Father, Son, and Holy Ghost." If the baby cried when being anointed with water it was said to be a sign of a good life.

On the journey home another tradition was carried out. The Godparent had a gift brought from home. It consisted of bread, cheese, and a piece of christening cake and a silver coin which had to be given to the first man she met on the way home from the church. It was given in the name of David, the new soul in our church. If the gift was accepted David would have good luck in life, if the gift was turned down the baby would be cursed. Fortunately I have never heard of anyone refusing a christening gift.

Back home a whisky toast was raised to our baby David. This was followed by the traditional snack of bread and cheese.

Then the cake was cut. For first babies this was the top layer of the wedding cake which was saved for this occasion. Small pieces of cake in special "christening boxes" were sent to family or friends who could not be at the ceremony. It was said that if an unmarried young woman slept with the piece of cake under her pillow she would dream of her own true love.

Much fuss was made over our baby David. It was usual to give a christening gift of silver coin to the new wee one. If it was grasped in the tiny hand it meant wealth and happiness. If the coin was dropped it meant bad luck.

"Babies don't thrive until they are christened," was the saying. Our baby sure thrived. After three girls, this was the son that Mum wanted. It was very important in those days to have a son to carry on the family name... Things settled down and we were one happy family.

FOODS - LIKES AND DISLIKES

8

When it came to food kids ate what was on the plate.......we had a good appetite and liked most foods......but I had two great dislikes.....beets and brussel sprouts. The beets were pickled in vinegar and I hated the sour taste.

One day, when Grandma Clark was having dinner with us she noticed my trouble with beets. "Oh, Dearie" she said "beets are good for you and will help you grow. I'll show you how to like them" She was right!!!!

Next time I ate at Grandma's there was one beet slice on the side of the plate. To please Grandma, I ate it first..... SURPRISE!!!!! It didn't have that awful vinegar taste (actually, there was just a taste of vinegar in my slice). Maybe I didn't love it, but it wasn't that bad.

Over the months she gradually introduced more vinegar until, after about six months, I could eat beets at full strength.

Grandma was so patient and calm you knew you could do what she asked of you. All my life I would not have vinegar on anything......but pickled beets I love.

No one could help me with Brussels sprouts.....we would have them in season, freshly picked from the garden.....usually for Sunday dinner. The call of "Dinner" from Mum brought us in from our play. The kitchen smelled of roast beef.....Oh, I was hungry. When we were settled round the table Mum put out the plates. Lovely roast beef, gravy, roasted potatoes and THREE UGLY GREEN EYEBALLS staring up at me from the plate I tried to ignore them as I worked my way round the roast beef. " Eat your Brussels sprouts" said mum. "I don't like them" "Well, you will eat them" said Mum, as I got the story of all the starving kids in the world salivating for my Brussels sprouts. I would have gladly have thrown them half way around the world to feed them.......but these were mine and had to be eaten by me.

We all knew the outcome here, everyone else finished dinner and the kids were excused to resume their play outside while I sat, with tears in my eyes. I should have forced them down first and been done with it, but I was only a kid and what did I know? The sprouts did not disappear, nor did they grow more appetizing as they grew cold.......eventually I had to eat them as fast as I could trying not to taste them. I'm sure this was as difficult for Mum as it was for me and we were both glad when brussel sprout season was over.

Later on, at Lawside Academy, some of the girls who had vacationed in France talked about eating snails in the restaurants there. "Oh, how horrible" I thought "How could anyone eat snails?" thinking of the fat slimy slugs I would see oozing over garden and path and imagining them sliced and on a plate made my taste buds cringe and my appetite disappear. They were far worse than Brussels sprouts.

Much later I learned that we Scots had all eaten snails, they were found in the nearby seas and were called whelks, otherwise known as "Wulks". The fisherwomen from Arbroath sold them at the door along with fresh fish. They sold a small bucketful for a few pennies. Also, at the bottom of the "Hilltown" was a women with a barrow who sold only "wulks". She supplied the straight pins to pick them out of their shells.

To quote Shakespeare "What's in a name? That which we call a rose by any other name would smell as sweet". Well, a snail by any other name really tasted good. Who would have guessed that our lowly "wulks" were really sea snails.

Our fast foods were the fish and chip shops and pie shops. I think they are called "take aways" now. They didn't cost very much and everything was freshly caught or made. We usually had a meat pie on washdays when Mum did not have time to cook. Made that day in Wallace's Pie Shop, they were delicious. Flaky, melt in your mouth pastry and full of minced meat.... YUM!!!!

The fish and chip shops, as I remember, opened around tea time (5 P.M.) staying open 'til late at night. The fish were freshly caught and delivered that day. They also sold chips (French Fries) and black or white puddings, which looked like large sausages and were fried in lard like the fish and chips. My favourite was black pudding that was just delicious..... until I found out years later that the correct name was "blood pudding", made from the blood of animals and I switched real fast to "white pudding" which was made from oatmeal.

The chip shop was always crowded, the menu always the same. Fish and chips or pudding and chips. The fish was always cod and the pudding Black or White. The front of the shop was quite small with a standing area for customers (no tables or chairs). A high counter, the other side of which had a cash register and a wrapping shelf with a supply of grease-proof paper squares and single pages of newspaper. Across from the shelf were two small vats of boiling lard, one for the fish and puddings and the other for chips. One person looked after the cooking while the other served. These were family businesses so we are mostly talking about the owner and his wife. They prepared the freshly caught fish and made the batter during the day so all was ready when "the hungry hordes" arrived.

Raw fish were dipped into a bucket of batter, then into the boiling lard, the fish and chips were constantly cooking to serve the constantly hungry customers. The fish and chip shop was a nice warm place on a cold night, it smelled pungently of fish, malt vinegar and boiling fat. The only sound was the sizzle of cooking food. After placing an order it seemed that hungry people were not in the mood for conversation...eating was all they had on their minds.

Another bonus from "The Chipper" was that the hot fish and chips kept your hands warm on the way home.

Everybody loved the fish and chips and also the pies from the bakery store and also Shepherd's pie and Cornish Pasties.

Our bakeries supplied every need for the "sweet tooth" which is the hallmark of all Brits. Cakes, Tarts, Trifle, Chocolates, and all kinds of confectionaries. We never gained weight from all these goodies and fried foods as we walked everywhere in all kinds of weather. Also, there was no "Tele" then and limited radio so we did not sit around much so we could well afford our diet and keep our trim figure at the same time.

WAR

9

Our family had settled down and everything seemed fine...but then there was something strange going on. It was kind of scary.....not the kind like bad dreams where Mum or Dad could make it better. This was different. All of the grown-ups had this strained look and we heard snatches of conversation...... Hitler...Germany....W A R!

As children we were not informed of what was wrong but this was a strange fear that seemed to affect everyone. One day, when David was just over two months old, the grown-ups were all down-stairs at Gran's gathered round the radio and the voice of Neville Chamberlain, our Prime Minister, announced that we were at war. The date was September 3rd 1939 and our lives were about to change drastically. Germany had broken it's non-aggression pact with Poland. Hitler was on the move in Europe and had just invaded. Britain and France had a pact with Poland to protect it's borders and when Poland was invaded we were at war. When Poland fell to the Nazis we knew that all of Europe including Britain would be in the fight of our lives.

In May of 1940 Winston Churchill was our newly appointed Prime Minister. In his first speech to The House of Commons on May 13th, 1940 he laid out his plan to the British people. He minced no words in his assessment of what lay ahead."I would say to "The House" as I said to those who have joined the government. I have nothing to offer but blood, toil, tears and sweat. We have before us an ordeal of the most grievous kind. We have many long months of struggle and suffering. You ask "What is our policy?" I say it is to wage war by land, sea and air. War with all the might and with all the strength God has given us, and to wage war against a monstrous tyranny never surpassed in the dark and lamentable catalogue of human crime. That is our policy. You ask "What is our aim?" I can answer in one word. It is victory. Victory at all costs. Victory in spite of all terrors - victory, however long and hard the road may be, for without victory there is no survival".

We were totally unprepared for war (wasn't the first world war "the war to end all wars?") But prepare we must and prepare we did. The authorities feared the mustard gas attacks of the 1918 war and one of the first things I remember was going to the big Kirk on Law Hill to be fitted for our gas masks. They were hot and smelly and awful but apart from some very scared little ones, there were no complaints, we all seemed to sense the seriousness of our predicament. Babies had to be laid in like a box made of heavy rubber with filters to keep out the gas.

All the men folk signed up immediately for service, we were going to be fighting for our survival. It must have been a logistical nightmare to become war-ready. There were less and less men around as they were trained, equipped and sent off to war. All our manufacturing was turned to the war effort. All able bodied women took over, making munitions, driving the buses, doing the laboring jobs. Grannies had to take over minding the kids. Though many children were evacuated out of the danger zones.

I remember that my two sisters and I were to be evacuated. David, still a baby was to stay at home with Gran. After waiting for weeks 'til buses became available, we were told to go to school for the evacuation. There were lots of crying kids with their little suitcases, bags and gas masks. The people in charge got our names from Mum, wrote them on large cardboard tickets with our new destination and tied them with string around our necks. We looked like the sorriest bunch of misplaced people and Mum, at the last minute, could not stand it. "Och! Ye can't take my bairns away from me" she said with that she got the tickets off us and we went HOME.

Many kids were evacuated although it was not mandatory. Remember that at that time most families lived closely in the same towns, so the evacuees went to live with strangers, mostly in small towns in the North or on farms in the country. There were stories about children being mis-treated or being used for farm labor and many came home after a short time.

Air-raid shelters were being built everywhere and the schools were being re- opened. We were issued identity cards which we had to have on us wherever we went. Same with the gas masks,

I remember that the authorities did drills and chose random streets in town to fill with tear gas. Anyone who didn't have their gas mask with them learned very quickly.

Food was in short supply, as were clothes. First priority was our servicemen and women, civilians had to learn to do without. The clothes part was real hard on growing children, so, hand-me-downs in clothes and shoes extended from families to neighbourhoods as we all learned to share. We had government issued clothes and food coupons but what you could buy was quite meagre.

I was at Gran's downstairs when I heard the first eerie rise and fall of our air-raid sirens. Gran's face held a look of terror, "they are after Leuchers air force base" she said. My uncles, HER SONS, along with many other men from Dundee were training at Leuchers which was across the river in Fife. We heard the bombers overhead, a few bombs were dropped but not much damage done and the Air Force Base was safe for now. Then we heard the sustained notes of the all clear.

Dad was spared going to war, he drove a street car and a few civilians were exempt. I surmise that being in his middle thirties, with four children and a wife with a serious heart problem may also have been the reason that he was exempt. He was in the ARP (Air Raid Patrol), had to patrol the street at night to make sure the law was obeyed, blackout precaution or accidents etc. Of course whenever the sirens sounded he was out on duty and, as for most families, we had to fend for ourselves.

Our part of town was high on Law Hill above the town. There was a large cave near the top of the hill ....it had been fitted with wooden benches along the sides of the cave and some electric lights and was considered safer than the man-made shelters. Most of our neighbourhood went there during the first few air raids, but it was so cold with water running down the inside of the walls. Mum decided to take her chances with the bombers rather having us all die of pneumonia so future raids found us all in Mum's big bed in the kitchen where we told jokes and sang songs 'til the all clear.

We could hear the German bombers and fighters overhead. The sound of their engines was unmistakable. Most times we heard them get louder as they came overhead and then the sound diminished as they went by. They were possibly after the dockyards on the Clyde or munitions depots or trains carrying troops and supplies. Dundee was situated in a valley, with the river Tay on one side and the Sidlaw hills on the other. The river Tay was over two miles wide at this point and there was always a mist which made the town more difficult to see from the air. Because of this, we did not get the fierce bombing of other towns. I do remember running for cover one afternoon. A couple of German fighters on the way back after a bombing raid strafed the streets as we were coming home from school.

As unprepared as we were for war, Britain was also preparing for an imminent invasion. Large poles were dug into our beaches to stop aircraft from landing. Our city center streets were covered in barbed wire to hinder easy access to our town government and businesses. Railings disappeared from all our parks and gardens, to be melted down for munitions. Our beautiful Law hill, where we gathered bluebells and made daisy chains and played in the soft grass, was now pock marked with concrete, squat, ugly machine gun nests called pill-boxes, necessary now for our defense. All ponds in town were emptied as the reflection of moon on water made night (when most raids took place) as clear as day. We all had to blackout our windows so no light shone through, with a heavy fine for discipline although everyone was very conscientious on this point. There were no street lights at night so we used flashlights which were hooded so that we just had a pinpoint of light to guide our feet, a good way to walk into and bruise ourselves on the sandbags which were everywhere to help cushion bomb blasts.

"Black- outs" was not just a matter of every household in the country being tightly controlled so that no light escaped. This was a matter of survival - most of the German raids took place during darkness and any light that would give knowledge of the land below would not only aid the enemy and be life-threatening to the people below but also help guide the bombers to their ultimate destination

Dundee in it's northern location was dark by 3 P.M. in the winter. In fact, on a rainy or snowy winter day it never really got light. When the sun did sometimes appear it hung low on the horizon, a dull dark red ball that appeared for only a few hours. So we had many hours in the day to deal with Black-Out.

First, there were the shops, from the corner little grocery stores to the big clothing and department stores or the large "five and dime" stores (like Woolworths). I remember all stores had to have double doors with a vestibule in between. You had to open the inside door, step into the vestibule, close the inside door so that you were in this dark space and then you could open the outside door to exit.... remember that no one could open the inside door while you were leaving. I would guess that one of the store employees had to manage the doors. (did they have to wait 'til there were quite a few leaving before they opened the outside doors?). I don't know how all of this was accomplished but, like everything else, we made it work.

Far bigger problem was our transportation. The buses and tramcars were used by most people for travel. The "British Medical Journal" reported at the end of 1939. "frightening the nation (Britain) with black-out regulations, the Luftwaffe was able to kill 600 citizens a month without even taking to the air"

The windows of our public transports were painted black so, once on board, you had no idea where you were and had to rely on the conductor to call out your destination. How did he know? Even standing on the dark entrance platform on the bus or tram what could he see? as the whole town was in darkness. Headlights on our transports were hooded so that the driver could see only a short distance in front. White lines painted in the centre of the street and curbs and trees did not do much to help nor did the luminous armbands that people wore. We also tried to wear something white in a traffic area but, even so, there were many accidents.

The speed limit for automobiles was 20 MPH, it didn't seem to help much as there were many road accidents with no guidance in the dark from familiar landmarks. On a cloudy or moonless night there were many reports of cars driving off bridges and also into lakes and other water hazards. I don't know if records were kept of all the road casualties during our five years of war. I would imagine it came nowhere near the bombing casualties, the road deaths were the lesser of two evils and the price we had to pay to confuse the enemy bombers.

Britain being an island, now being circled by U-boats to stop any supplies of food from getting through and most of what we did grow going directly to our troops, we did have a problem. All the parks and gardens were dug up for food plots (victory gardens) and we all had to grow most of our own food. Nothing was wasted. All leftovers (very little of that) and potato and vegetable peelings went into the "pigs bins" to feed livestock. This was mandatory with heavy penalties for non-compliance.

Lord Haw Haw was on the radio continually. He would broadcast messages about certain cities that had been badly bombed, with many casualties. ALL LIES. One day our town got the treatment from this traitor. He mentioned three schools in town that had taken direct hits and that hundreds of children had been killed. We thought it was very funny as nothing had happened in Dundee and we knew it, then Mum pointed out that the broadcast was going to our men in the war and they had no way of knowing what was true. These radio broadcasts from Germany were meant to stress our fighting men who had no way of knowing if their families were dead or injured. These schools had been mentioned by name and that made it seem more real.

Within a short time all the abnormalities became a way of life and we adapted. With all the shelters in place, the schools opened again and we got used to all the rationing. The adults were glued to the news which was not good for Britain for the first couple of years. As a nine year old girl, my biggest problem was sitting through the raids in a dark air raid shelter next to a little boy I had a crush on. There was much giggling and teasing and blushing going on.

MORE ON WAR

10

During "the War" (world war two....1939-1945) we learned to do without many things that had been taken for granted. All manufacturing was turned to the war effort. Companies that had made children's clothes and fashions for women were now making uniforms and sturdy boots for men in battle, and parachutes for our brave airmen. Manufacturers of household goods were now making guns and shells, of which we needed a constant supply. Blankets, pillows, beds, things needed for everyday living, were diverted to our troops. Buses and ambulances were also commandeered and sent where they were needed. Doctors, nurses and dentists were in short supply on the home front as our troops had need of them.

I was almost eleven when Mum sent me to help a grandmother next door. Her grandson had fallen and injured his chin which was bleeding and possibly needed some stitches. Middle of the afternoon and no adults around, Mum was busy with my baby brother. I had burned my foot the previous year and was well acquainted with the hospital, so was sent as a help and a guide.

As we entered the emergency waiting room, a huge, dark and dreary place, we had a long wait 'til someone could come to see us (most of our doctors and nurses were serving our country and were in short supply for the civilian population). There were two other people in the huge waiting room, a soldier in uniform and a little girl about six years old who was lying on one of the benches and wrapped in a blanket. "Don't come near" said the soldier and, as we took our seat at the other end of the room he called out again " My wee lass has diphtheria and we are waiting for an ambulance to take her to our Sanitarium" (in those days all infectious diseases were kept apart from the general population). No doctor or nurse came near the little girl for fear of carrying the disease to others so she and her father waited and, I'm sure, prayed for that ambulance to arrive soon. At the Sanitarium visitors were not allowed inside and had to visit thru' closed glass windows. All deliveries were left outside the front door so that there was no contact with the outside world.

King's Cross Hospital was absolute in it's quarantine. I remember the early forties, when we had a smallpox outbreak, the six or so patients were confined. One mother insisted that she be allowed to be with her sick young daughter, of course, she was not allowed to leave 'til the disease had run it's course. The daughter recovered, but, unfortunately, her mother caught smallpox and died.

Back to us in the emergency room. Our little boy eventually was evaluated and had his wound seen to, stitches, as we thought.

As we were leaving a good two hours later, the soldier and his wee, very sick daughter were still awaiting an ambulance. There were many tragic events during the war years that we were not aware of.

Sadness also that there was that we did see. A favorite neighbor was missing. We no longer would see her on our daily walks ,or at the bakery vans, or at the grocer's store. After about three weeks she appeared, had lost so much weight and her eyes were all red and puffed up from crying. People were so quiet and gentle around her. Her husband was off at the war front and she had just lost her 18 year old son - her only child - on some distant mission.

We could not dwell for too long on sadness, we were fighting for survival in a war we had to win. The pictures (movies) were very popular, the light musicals of the times were a great diversion and did not cost much. Of course you were turned away if you did not have your gas mask and identity card. Luckily the feared gas attacks did not happen, though we still had to carry our masks but all we had to worry about were the bombing raids. When the sirens would warn of a raid, the drill was always the same. Picture off, emergency lights went on, everyone stayed in their seats, music came on, words and the bouncing ball appeared on the screen and we sang until the "all clear" when the picture would resume. Yes, we sure got our money's worth at the pictures some nights.

Communities were now closer than ever as we tried to share and help each other out. I remember a young couple, she seventeen and he who at eighteen had just been called to duty. News spread that they were getting married before he left for war. And the street rallied around them. In short order neighbours donated wedding dress and veil, also food coupons and many helping hands - a banquet was prepared and a wedding cake made. Gardeners from all around brought flowers from their allotments. Someone brought huge white wedding bells that they had saved. Taking down the clotheslines from the huge drying green in the middle of the biggest of the flats, it became a lovely wedding garden. Forgetting about war and worries and lack of money, we all went to a wedding. Love was in the air, as was hope for the future.

There was also another more sinister side to the war years. Our "bobbies" the men in blue who kept law and order in our town and neighbourhood were greatly depleted as all able bodied men were called to duty. There are many wonderful people in this world but for every positive there is a negative and there were people who were up to no good. As men aged seventeen thru' their fifties were shipped out, we had a great population of women, many young, with little children to care for, who were alone and unprotected.

Case in point, my cousin Robert was serving in the Air Force. His wife Evelyn, an attractive young woman in her early twenties with two children aged one and three, lived in a ground floor flat. She had gone across "the backies" (joined backyard) to borrow something from a friend one evening, her children asleep in bed, she was gone only five minutes. On her way home in the dark a man lunged out from the shadows and tried to grab her. Fear and desperation made her strong and she managed to get away and run for her apartment, the man running close behind. Reaching home she slammed the door shut and bolted it just in time. A man's voice came at her thru' the door. "I know you are in there and you are alone, I'll find a way to get in". What was Evelyn to do? There were no home phones or cell phones, no electronic means of communication in those days. She used the only means of communication that she had. Luckily, her upstairs neighbors were home as she heard their radio playing - taking her kitchen broom she banged on the ceiling to get their attention, the radio went off, and an answering broom to the floor told her they had heard her. She yelled as loudly as she could "rapist at door - HELP". There was shouting, and banging on doors as neighbors alerted others - the sound of heavy footsteps as women with brooms and fireside pokers ran to do battle with the intruder, remember that there were no able bodied men around, and guns were not even carried by our policemen.

Of course, there was no one there when they got downstairs. Babies were now awake and crying and some of the older women helped calm them back to sleep. Then they stayed for a couple of hours until Evelyn herself had calmed down, they were helped by that institution which comforted all Scottish women "A nice cup of tea and a biscuit".

FAMILY

11

Earliest history of my home town of Dundee began in the Iron age in seventh century A.D. with an ancient tribe called The Picts. Later, during the Medieval era there were many battles fought near the city and for protection it became a walled city in 1545, the many districts being known by the various gates. There was the Sea Gate, the Well Gate, the Overgate, the East Gate and the West Gate. Dundee grew to become the fourth largest city in Scotland and walls and gates were a thing of the past but the names now denote the different areas in town.

Families lived close to each other within the districts. We lived at "the tap o' the hill" otherwise known as the Hilltown (no gates here as we were high on Law Hill and protected by the city below) and were within fifteen minutes walk of each other.

Grannie and Granpa Spiers lived downstairs from us as did Uncles Bob, Joe, John and Jim with cousins Anna, Grace, John, May and Dougie. Auntie Belle and uncle Bob lived at the top of

Hilltown with cousins Betty, Anna, Robert and Ina. Auntie Chris and Uncle Dave lived on Caldrum Street (near The Steamie) with cousins Maisie, Jean, Isobel and May. Uncle Dave and Aunt Jean lived at the further edge of town with three cousins at a place named Lochee. I don't remember the names of those cousins, we did not see them often. Maybe once a year when we had our yearly picnic to the beach, we went by train.

Gran's house was always full of action and noise and Gran was so busy from morning 'til night looking after all of the clan who lived with her. She did manage occasionally to have a night at "the pictures", she took only one person with her and that was one of the grandkids. We enjoyed some special time with Gran and she had a nice rest.

I should mention at this time that "the pictures" was our favorite choice of entertainment. Hilltown had three movie theatres, the Odeon, the Regent and the Empire, the movies were a great treat when the weather was cold and windy and wet (which was most of the year). Shirley Temple was a favorite as were Ginger Rogers and Fred Astaire musicals, we had the usual cartoons, Mickey and Minnie, Bugs Bunny and Porky Pig. Our comedians were Laurel and Hardy, The Marx Brothers and Red Skelton (I thought it was Red Skeleton and wouldn't go to what I thought was a scary movie). Of course there was Frankenstein and Dr Jekyll and Mr Hyde, the Hunchback of Notre Dame, Phantom of the Opera and The Picture of Dorian Gray to scare us. These were all black and white pictures. There was quite a stir when "Snow White came out in 1938... it was the first full length animated film and was also in Technicolour.

It was sixpence for a movie and kids got in for half price with an adult. When Mom and Dad wanted a little time to themselves they kept "the wee ones" at home and sent Betty and I to the pictures. We got threepence each for admission. When we got to the theatre queue, we checked the people in line, and chose a man and woman, usually with kids of their own. "Will ye tak' us into the pictures?". As this was a ploy most parents used at some time, the answer would be "Gie us y'er money". When we reached the ticket office they would ask for two adults and XX halves. Once inside they would give us our ticket stubs and with a "thanks missus" we were off to find our seats and enjoy the movie.

Busy as she was, Gran Spiers never forgot a birthday we had no extra money for parties and gifts but she always managed a cake from the bakery and candles. We would all gather round the table and sing "happy birthday" Boy! we sure were loud.

I remember that she gave Hallowe'en parties for us kids, dunking for apples in the deep galvanized bath tub, we told ghost stories around the fire in the dark, Gran hovering nearby and giving us a hug every now and again. When the lights were turned on we all had soot on our faces (from our hovering Gran), we played other games. The clothes pulley had strings attached, scones were attached about kid height, said scones dripping with treacle. We had to keep our hands behind our backs and eat the scone assigned to us while getting treacle (molasses) slapping all over our face and in our hair. For winning, we had only bragging rights and that was enough. Gran soaked wash cloths in cold water from the tap and we each cleaned the sticky goop from our faces....it was such good fun with lots of noise and laughter.

Grandma and grandpa Clark lived in a "But and Ben" (room and kitchen) in Reid Street, about half a mile from us. So different from Mum's family. There was just the two of them and their wee dog Dinkie (a wire haired terrier). One thing about their kitchen was special, it was like all the other apartments in the building, window facing out to the drying greens and gray buildings all around. We often had cloudy skies especially in the winter months and everything seemed to be gray, except for one thing..... grandma had paper cut-outs of five beautiful blue-birds in the top corner of her window. Her son Harry worked in the grocery store nearby and the bluebirds had been a store display, Uncle Harry brought them home when the store was done with them and grandma pasted them on the window. They did not have much in material things but there was always beauty in grandma's house. It was lovely, in winter, if it had been snowing and everything was white and gray outside, the bluebirds were the first thing in your sight.

All was orderly and quiet at grandma's house, family visited on regular basis but not all at once like at Gran's. Uncle John started a business and lived in England with Aunt Alice, they had no children. He visited a couple of times a year, had a model T car and was quite prosperous. Aunt Aggie lived on Hilltown with Uncle John and cousins Cath, Peggy and Mary. Uncle Harry and Auntie Agnes live on Hill street, a quarter mile away, with cousins Alison and Phil. Uncle Jim and Aunt Mary lived on Kinloch street with cousins Hugh and James.(Mom and Dad lived there when I was born) Auntie Cath and uncle Alf lived in Lochee with cousins Elinor and Alfred. Aunt Cath came to Gran's every Friday as they got older, did shopping and cleaning and then we had a special high tea with small sandwiches and cakes.

I was always invited as I was her favorite niece. She was at my birth and said she fell in love with me then and loved me until the day she died at 93 years old (that was a lot of loving) of course we had a special bond and and I loved her dearly. Auntie Mae and Uncle Harry lived near Dens Park (our soccer stadium) with two cousins (can't remember their names. We were all within walking distance of each other.

As I said, Grandma Clark's was quietly and calmly in order, nothing house proud or strict, just comfortable and kind and loving. If our family visited on Saturday evening we would see that Grandma had everything ready for Sunday Mass. Sunday clothes pressed and brushed. Grandpa had shined the shoes and they were as black and shiny as shoes could be. Gran's hat and gloves, prayer book and rosaries were laid out and they always set out in plenty of time for a leisurely walk to church...no rushing or panic like at our house.

Catholic Church in the thirties was very strict and regimental and scary to a little kid. Not allowed to sit with our parents, we had to sit in front with all the other schoolchildren, boys on one side, girls on the other, under the watchful eyes of our teachers, who made sure we didn't talk or move except at the assigned times. It was so stern and restricting knowing God would punish us if we did not behave.

One day, when I was about five or six I had been downtown to the shops with Grandma...her last stop at the bakery where she bought some cookies. Going home was tiring... a steep climb up Hilltown and Gran could see that I was getting tired. Halfway up was our St Mary's Catholic church "Let's go into St Mary's for a minute" says Gran.

We blessed ourselves from the "holy water" at the entrance. The church was huge to me, dark, with 'Stations of the Cross' on one side, flickering prayer and penance candles lit in front and statues looking down on me (to see that I behaved, I thought). I genuflected as I had been taught, and went straight down on my knees on the hard wooden risers, also as I had been taught. It was so quiet and not a soul around. I felt Gran's hand on my shoulder as she whispered "Sit back on the pew dearie" I did as I was told....oh!, it was so good to sit down. Staring straight ahead, I closed my eyes to pray (felt guilty not kneeling). Soft rustling next to me, Granma holding out a bag. "Have a cookie, dearie" I froze, thinking God would strike me down for not behaving in church "Grandma, I can't... WE ARE IN CHURCH". She said something I have remembered for a lifetime "dearie, we are in God's house and God is our Father... surely he would have us rest in His house if we were tired and eat if we were hungry" It was so simple to Gran, if you loved someone you took care of them. Gran wasn't raised Catholic and became so after marrying grandpa. Of course, I rested and enjoyed my cookie and we left and went on our way refreshed. I just enjoyed the moment then, but, looking back on it, I had just received the best sermon in the world from my sweet, humble, loving Scottish Grandmother.

Birthday parties at Granma Clark's house came complete with paper hats and party crackers that snapped when you pulled them and had a little prize inside. No birthday cake, granma always made a "cloutie dumplin'" with lucky charms in it, the big prize being one silver threepenny bit. These were all wrapped in a little wax paper before being put into the pudding mix before cooking. Granma's pudding was delicious but you had to be careful you didn't bite into or swallow a prize (that was part of the fun)

We could always find granma and granpa Clark summer evenings walking their dog "Dinkie" on their leisurely walks round the "ringie roadie", the wide road that circled Law Hill meadows. It was about three miles in circumference which brought them back home. At one point the road overlooked all of Dundee and the river Tay below, also our railroad bridge over the river. Tay bridge was built in 1878, it was 2.75 miles long and, at that time, the longest railway bridge in Europe. It became infamous nineteen months later, at 7.15 P.M. on December 28th 1879, when the middle section of the bridge collapsed during a fierce winter storm taking the train and passengers into the river below. All 75 passengers and crew died.

In a large and loving family we were dearly loved by both grandmas. Both were so different in their personalities and their lives. Gran Spiers (mum's) was busy almost every moment 'til the day she died.

After granpa died she had the responsibility for four uncles and five cousins. Always too busy to see a doctor or take care of herself if she felt ill, she always worked through colds, bronchitis and assorted ills. She was so sick one night that a doctor had to be called, when he visited, it was too late, and gran died of pneumonia the next day.

As was the custom at that time, after she was prepared for burial Gran was brought home a few days before the funeral and the coffin placed in the furthest corner of the main room.

Death in the midst of life, and life in the midst of death. We kids could see grannie and mourn her but all seemed so normal, as meals were made, and eaten, tables were set, dishes washed and fire tended to, bed slept in and babies fed and grannie was home amidst her family, where she lived and loved.

Neighbors including children living nearby visited to pay their respects. There was an extra step by the side of the casket so the wee ones could see Gran and pay their respects. Gran was never too busy for all the kids and if they needed something she was there to dry their tears or get them some bread and jam. And they came to Gran's house to say goodbye. So we learned at an early age that death was part of life.

MUM'S ILLNESS

12

When David was a little over three years old, Dad called us in from play one day. Mum was out with my little brother visiting Gran who lived in the flat downstairs.

Dad was a kind, gentle, man with a sense of humour that delighted us, but on this occasion he was more serious than I had known in my young life. "Things are going to change for us" he said "your Mum has a heart condition and she cannot do all the work needed to look after us" We were scared, we didn't know what a heart condition was but from Dad's manner it was serious.

When I was an adult I learned that Mum had Rheumatic Fever when she was a child. After she recovered all was well, or so everyone thought. However, it wasn't known in those days that the fever could damage the heart. When Mum was pregnant with David it was discovered that her heart valves had been damaged. Doctors told her that giving birth could cause much damage to the already burdened heart and wanted to terminate the pregnancy. But Mum would not hear of it. First of all, we were Roman Catholic and second, this might be the son that Mother hoped for. Well, Mother got her son and we got our little brother but things did change.

After a few years Mum did not have the strength she used to have and each year that passed took away her ability to do the hard work needed to look after a family with four kids. Money was scarce since there must have been doctor and hospital bills to pay, but we were never told of them. The Scots are a very proud and independent people so there was no asking for help, although, money wise everyone was living week to week so Dad made the best he could out of our situation. I had the job, on occasion, to visit the local pawn shop. It was in the poorest part of town, the Overgate, up a long narrow alleyway, with three brass balls out front. I was so ashamed and was careful that no one saw me. Dad's Sunday suit brought us one pound cash and when Dad got his pay I reclaimed the suit. I'm sure this was normal for many in Dundee at that time but was kept very quiet.

By the time I was thirteen and Bette was eleven, we had to take on all of the housework. We had always been very responsible and had always had household chores to do, as had many of our friends, but this was a heavy load for us. Dad couldn't take time off from work as we lived from week to week in the best of times. All of the immediate family had family of their own to care for, most of the mothers held down some kind of work to augment their family income (mostly in the jute mills) and grandmothers had many children to care for as their parents worked.

Family helped where they could but as a family we had to become self sufficient. Mum could still look after baby and do some light cooking but she tired easily and had to rest often.

We had to divide up the chores.... Shopping was an everyday thing as we had little storage and no refrigeration. Mum could still go to the little shop at the bottom of the lane. However, our bakeries, fish shops, butchers and greengrocers were about a mile away, at the top of the Hilltown. This also was where the tram stopped before going downtown to City Centre and also to the edge of town at Downfield. There were no buses or trams in our neighbourhood.

Dundee was on a hill. Law Hill was almost six hundred feet above sea level and the town was built around it. We lived high up on the hill so we went downhill to the shops and then had an uphill climb home. This was too much for Mum's ailing heart. We girls were now nine, eleven and thirteen respectively and Dad could pick up some groceries on his way home from work so shopping was not too much of a problem.

The lighter chores we girls had been doing for many years such as dusting, dishes, cleaning the brasses every week, including our brass nameplate and letter slot on the door. These were always kept bright and shiny and were a source of pride.

The heaviest chores were the scrubbing and the laundry, which were given to Betty and me. As Betty was taller and stronger than I she was given the responsibility of the weekly wash. A tremendous task for a child not quite twelve years old. Of course, she could not do what Mum did in the washhouse, but she could go to our "Steamie". Minimum age was fourteen as that was school graduation age but Betty looked older than her years and no one questioned her. You were not restricted to one day a week, so Betty could do smaller loads, however, I think it cost about sixpence an hour so we had to watch our pennies.

First task was getting the clothes to the wash-house. Wear your oldest, most comfortable clothes and a cloth turban on your head to keep your hair dry from the steam. We lived a little over a mile uphill from Caldrum Street, the location of the "Steamie".

Preparation, dirty clothes were wrapped in sheets, washboard and soap on top and put into David's old pram (perambulator), with it's wheels and a handle, it was easy pushing downhill. The return journey uphill needed much more heavy work. Betty was strong and healthy but wash days were really tiring for someone of her age. However, being a kid, she just needed a good strong cup of tea and a piece of cake for re-fueling and she was out playing with her friends.

For sixpence an hour you could rent a cubical which had a boiler, sinks, and running hot and cold water. There were also communal "extractors" (a kind of spin dryer). Also with your cubical came your own heated drying rods, after hanging your slightly wet clothes over the rods, the whole contraption was slid into a heated wall cupboard where your clothes dried in record time. No worry about the cold or the rain here. After your allotted time you had to clean up and leave the cubical spotless for the next renter.

Betty's thirteenth birthday happened to be on a wash day. She was so pleased to be a teenager. She told me "I told the lady it was my birthday and I nearly gave myself away. I remembered in time to say that I was "fifteen" as I had been at the "Steamie" for over a year and was not even yet the proper age ".

I was responsible for a clean house, this included keeping the floors scrubbed and sparkling......No mops or any helps...Wash basin, soap, scrubbing brush and rinsing and drying....it was quite a job on hands and knees. Thank goodness our house was not too big!

I also had to take our "turn at the stairs". "The stairs" in our tenements and apartments were "common properties" and the responsibility of the tenants. We were on the top floor of our two story building and shared these duties with Mrs Milton, who lived next door. We took turns week about, sweeping every day and scrubbing once a week.

We had the landing by our doors and about fifteen steps to "the close" which was the responsibility of the downstairs neighbours. The Scots are not shirkers when it comes to hard work and take a pride in their environment.

Kettle on stove to heat water so I started out with hot water in my bucket. Of course, the cold outside and the cold stone steps soon had the water cold and dirty, so I replaced the water with clean and hot halfway through (heating water on stove). Being open to the elements, usually cold, windy and damp, not only was the water cold and dirty but also the washer. No pads on the stairs to cushion knees as it would just be a nuisance moving them and they would get wet anyway.

Steps were cleaned same as the floor at home, slosh with water, then soap and scrub then rinse and dry. An extra finishing touch was used....some kind of tablet to smooth over clean steps to whiten them (tops and sides). It took over an hour and looked really good when finished. That was until folks started using the stairs. But it was nice for a while and we knew that the stairs had been cleaned.

This started when Betty was eleven and I thirteen and we were still schoolgirls. By the age of fourteen and sixteen respectively we were both out of school and had full time jobs but our main chores were the same. No one complained, we just did what had to be done. We were part of a large, close and loving family and had a happy home life.

EVERYDAY NEEDS

13

There were many social aspects to living in our little two room cold water flats. Apart from the neighbors, we also had many commercial visitors.

Never was a check written in our little community. No one had a bank account. Workers were paid cash (in little envelopes showing hours worked) which didn't stay in hand for long. Everyone lived from week to week - that was the way it was - as long as your pay lasted 'til Thursday you were all right when pay day came around again. Our needs were simple, our family close and loving, it made for an uncomplicated and happy life.

We had weekly visits from the rent man. He always came round on Saturday (Friday being pay day) and was always paid in cash, he duly noted in his little book that we were paid for the week. For our lighting and cooking we used gas, there was a gas meter in the kitchen cupboard and we had to put a penny in the slot as needed.

If we ran out of money for the meter the result was instant....we ran out of gas. Cooking would stop immediately and light would go out. Then we would have to borrow from family downstairs.

The familiar call of "COAL" meant that the coalman was on his rounds. He always reminded me of a chimney sweep being black all over from the coal dust(even his eyelids) and wore a heavy leather shield on his back and heavy leather gloves. He had a wooden cart pulled by a Clydesdale horse. I remember the horse standing quietly by the entrance with it's breath misting in the cold winter air. These were huge beasts of burden, not the pampered and groomed ones that we see in parades today. The cart was filled with jute sacks full of coal. The shout of "COAL" up the stairwell brought the neighbors out to call down their orders. Mum usually got one or two bags. Coalman would heave the heavy bag onto his shoulders, climb the stairs, come into the kitchen, and empty the coal into the bunker by the sink. This was to heat the whole house until the coalman returned. Some days of heavy snow he would be late, but he always managed to make it through and, as the fire died out and the house became very cold, the familiar shout of "COAL" was a life saver. So many people depended on the lowly coalman.

We also had visits from "Indian Johnny", our pedlar man. He was an honest-to-goodness Indian from the exotic country of India, with a swarthy complexion and a turban on his head. The large suitcase he carried held many things - cheap perfume, face powder for the young ladies and playing cards for the men folk and an assortment of hankies and scarves. His wares didn't cost much and we always had a few pennies to spare when "Indian Johnny" came by.

Fisherwomen from the neighbouring fishing villages were visitors too. Big buxom lasses wearing the black and white striped aprons which identified them. They sold smoked haddock (finnan haddie) and fresh fish which they carried in wicker baskets on their backs.

We also had small shops on every street corner, which we really relied on, remember folks all lived in crowded coldwater flats so there were lots of people buying everyday necessities. These shops were run by families and it was hard work. Only day they closed was Sunday, all other days they opened at 5.30 A.M. when they took their first delivery of morning rolls. No one could go to work or school without our usual Scottish breakfast....two fresh rolls slathered with either butter or jam and a very hot, very strong cup of tea. Oatmeal, or porridge, as we Scots called it, was usually a lunch meal. It took forever to cook as "instant" was un-heard of, you had to stir the porridge constantly or you had lumpy porridge so it took some time to cook. Stores did not close 'til 9 P.M. Did you need silk stockings? or socks for the kids, cookies, baked goods, throat lozenges, face powder candies, gas mantles, writing paper, soaps, bulk syrup and treacle from the big barrels? prices had to be reasonable, remember this was a poor neighbourhood....so our shopkeepers did not live much better than their customers.

The bakery, for a fee would deliver morning rolls to your door every day. My older cousin, John, who was about eleven or twelve, delivered rolls before school and one morning he let me go on his rounds with him. Had to get up real early 5AM. Gran was already up, had replenished the fire and the kitchen was warm and cozy. She had tea and toast ready for us (no rolls at this hour). Toast was made by impaling the bread on a huge three-prong fork which was held against the grate of the fire and then turned to toast both sides. It was O.K.

First we went to the bakery where orders were in two baskets with names attached to each order. John knew most of the customers by heart as he had delivered for about six months. Remember that most folks in our area lived in tenements three or four stories high and climbing the cold, dark stairs ceased to be fun after the first few deliveries. Then back to check in with the bakery, return baskets, walk home, have breakfast and then start school for the day. On Saturday morning around 10AM John had to collect from the customers and sometimes got a few pennies in tips which he could keep. The bakery money went to the household as everyone had to contribute.

Milkman delivered our dairy products daily. And the butcher shop sold only meat. The carcasses were hanging by hooks on a rail in the shop, with sawdust on the floor to absorb any blood splatters. When you ordered your meat butcher hoisted the carcass onto his counter and hacked the piece out as you watched. I know that seems so primitive but it was all so normal to us, and I never heard of anyone getting sick from the meat, maybe the cold Scottish weather had a lot to do with it.

Shopping took quite a bit of time. With no refrigeration and little storage space, groceries were bought every day so our little neighborhood shops and our pedlars were really needed.

THE ACADEMY

14

I was growing up. When I was twelve I had won a silver medal for Scottish Folk Singing with a chance to compete the following year for the gold medal. That year I was also awarded a scholarship to our Catholic Academy, which was a stepping stone to eventual university.

We had three academies in Dundee and they were reserved for the upper class in our stratified society. In the Scottish education system of that day the dividing line was as we reached the age of twelve. School leaving age (graduation) was fourteen. Students usually progressed to our high school, where the boys were taught a trade and the girls were taught cooking, secretarial work and general studies. As I said before, Dundee was a jute town so most of our high school graduates ended up working in the shops around town, or working in the mills. The jute mills hired mostly women, who worked the looms, while the men did laboring and maintenance work.

Our academies covered the years through age sixteen and were the only access to the Universities. They had the best of facilities, music rooms, science labs, art studios and the finest of teachers - the kids of V.I.P.s and quite wealthy people in our society paid to attend the academies where they were well taught to excel at University and eventually take their place in the upper circles of our stratified society. However, each academy, annually, thru' a rigorous exam, chose a few of the lower working class to educate, (noblesse oblige). I was one of about five students from our Catholic schools to attend Lawside, our Catholic academy.

Mom and Dad were so proud, as a scholarship was an honor to working folk. They sacrificed clothing coupons (this was wartime) and money to outfit me with the school uniforms required. All else was supplied by my scholarship. In my new school I associated with children of V.I.P.s in town who grew up in privilege I couldn't imagine. The uniforms were bought at the one store in town - they were all the same quality and style so that leveled the playing field somewhat and I did not feel out of place in the classroom.

We studied Science, Literature, French, Latin, higher Math, Art and Music..... and learned to play tennis and field hockey. We were also taught responsibility, and pride in our school as we were recognized by our uniforms and the honor of the school rested on our shoulders.

Lawside was of high academic standard according to the Scottish Education System. Our difference from the other academies, we being Catholic, was that our school was within the walls of the convent of the "Sisters of Mercy" and we had religious studies class every day. We had the best of teachers, all Catholic, some being nuns of the convent.

Our principal, Sister Mary Joseph, was an excellent math teacher in her own right. She did not teach, however, being principal of the school and always seemed distant and strict to us - never a smile and soooo serious. However, she took over our math class in an emergency one day. We were all in fear of the strict, serious and judgmental principal. Surprise!, upon entering our class she was no longer Head Mistress but a warm, kind, excellent teacher, who took great pains to make sure everyone understood the basics of our study. She, as a teacher, was an entirely different person. Apart from Math, I learned a great lesson about judging people. I did well in my first year, I loved French and excelled at it, also did well in my other studies......loved singing, after all, remember I told you about my father's lovely tenor voice, also my mother was a good soprano and most of her family sang.... no trained voices, after all, we were working folks but when the family got together (which was most of the time) the auld Scots songs got quite a melodious airing. These were in the days before TV, and, although we had a radio which ran on a very heavy acid battery which had to be re-juiced quite often, the BBC broadcast only a few hours a day so most entertainment was within the family at get-togethers.

I loved my first year at Lawside Academy - however, Mum's heart problems were now showing themselves. In my second year at Lawside if Mum couldn't cope with my young brother, now about four, she would keep me home to look after things so she could rest. It didn't help - my taking the time off - and also trying to study at the kitchen table in our small two room flat. I was on my own with schoolwork, no one that I knew had any idea of French, Science or Literature etc., my friends at school were scholarship kids and had no support either.

First April at Lawside, that time of year came around for the Leng Gold medal Competition in Scots Folk Songs. In my all girl class (age 12 thru' 13, sexes still had separate classes and recess), there was one other girl and myself to compete in the big hall downtown. The other girl was one of my privileged classmates, an only child and her father owned the biggest business in town.

She had all that money and privilege could buy. While we went camping at Carnoustie, she vacationed, before the war, with her family in Europe. When it came to our Leng Gold Medal competition, she always had private elocution, voice and ballet lessons and all I had was the voice the good Lord had given me. Our music teacher worked with us on a song of her choosing from the list of Scottish Folk Songs supplied from the competition committee. I remember that I didn't have a decent coat to wear as we had used the last of our money and coupons on a coat for my younger sister who was a little taller that I (I was such a wee thing). So Mom solved the problem by giving me my sister's new coat for the occasion. I don't blame Betty for being mad at me. A new coat was so special and to have me wearing it was hurtful, thinking Mom was playing favorites. Mom, for her part, couldn't have me at such an occasion in an old coat. We were not allowed to wear our school uniforms. There was fierce competition, especially among the three academies in town and nobody wanted to be accused of favoritism.

The hall was huge and packed, there must have been almost six hundred adults in the audience. Some very important people in the town, the Scots took their musical heritage very seriously.

The first few rows were filled with nervous competitors. I competed against sixty other Silver Medalists from all the schools in town, aged twelve thru' sixteen and I didn't stand a chance. The stage seemed so big and high, the accompanist at one side at a grand piano. In front of us were five judges, well known in musical circles in the area. When my name was called, I don't know how I got up on that stage... but I did. The accompanist smiled that smile of encouragement he gave to all the competitors. The music started and I sang as I had been taught at school. We waited thru' all the others (it was a long evening).Then it was announced that two girls were tied for first place and would have to sing again... Surprise! Surprise!, I was one of the top two......up on the stage again...smile of encouragement....my teacher was excellent and had taught me well. I remembered all that she had taught me. AND I WON!!!! At twelve years of age, one of the youngest and the smallest became the Gold Medalist that year. I had brought honor to my school.

As we went home on the tramcar that night, people would come over to talk to "the wee lass that won the medal". Our first stop was at Gran and Gramps(dad's side) to give them the news. On the way there we stopped at the fish and chip shop. I usually got chips while the grown-ups got the fish but on this night I GOT A FISH SUPPER. I'll always remember that and thinking to myself "Maybe there is something to this singing"....in later years "this singing" was to bring me to my darling husband.

Beginning day at school never varied. When the bell rang we all assembled in our classes on the quadrangle. We stood in silence as Sister Mary Joseph said the morning prayers and gave out any announcements. First day of school after I won the medal I was surprised by the announcement "Anna Clark of "? House" has won for us the Leng Gold Medal in singing and I ask her to come and sing for us her Scottish song". Much whooping and clapping as I mounted the steps to stand beside our Principal to sing my song a cappella. I should have been proud, but I was just embarrassed to be singled out in front of my classmates.

One other memory of my school years was our class rebellion. First I must tell you of our uniforms. They were all the same style and quality, bought from the student store in town and consisted of: White blouses, long and short sleeve: Tie in the school colours, (wide navy blue with narrow light blue and yellow stripes): Navy blue tunic, knee length with pleated skirt: school colours on square neckline of tunic and also on the waistline: long black woolen stockings: black lace-up shoes: navy blue wool winter coat: long wool scarf in school colours: navy blue blazer with school emblem on upper pocket: navy blue brimmed hat with school emblem.

The uniforms were no problem except for the long black wool stockings which were mandatory summer and winter. They were restricting, scratchy and just plain, old ugly and besides, we were supposed to deport ourselves as young ladies, but we felt like little kids in our heavy woolen stockings. Looking at both sides, being a Roman Catholic school, modesty was very important.

The class leaders held a meeting after hours and, after putting it to a vote, decided to take action. Since trying to approach our head mistress did not work (she would not even listen to our request for a meeting) it was decided that Sister would have to approach US in this matter. It would take the action of the whole class and Sister would have to react to us.

Monday morning was exciting and scary. I felt naked as I walked to school in my light wool navy SHORT socks (bought at the uniform store so they were all the same). The other students in the school yard wondered what was going on but, as decided at our class meeting, we said nothing. The assembly bell rang and we lined up in silence in our classes. Such a mixture of emotions as our rebellion became apparent. Our head mistress, also a nun of the "Sisters of Mercy" order, looked to me like the avenging angel in her flowing black robes and heavy crucifix and beads. As she walked onto the steps facing the quadrangle, she stopped as she took in the scene. Our rebellion was obvious. She then said "Let us pray", led us in our morning prayers and then gave the announcements of the day. IS SHE GOING TO JUST IGNORE US????? Then quietly and firmly she said "I want to see the two prefects from year two girls in my office immediately".

Our prefects were not only of the privileged class, they were popular and likable. Not only that, they were both very articulate and persuasive. They brought to the discussion the fact that it cost twice as many clothing coupons for the long stockings which had to be replaced quite a few times a year.

This took away the clothing options for other members of a family (remember that this was war time). Explained in these terms, sister was gracious and allowed us to wear short socks DURING THE SUMMER ONLY. Sister was still in charge but we felt that we had won.

I was not quite three years at the academy, my mum had a heart condition, there were medical bills to pay. I was the eldest in the family and had to bring in a paycheck to help with finances. Seven months after my fourteenth birthday Dad sent a note to school that I should terminate the academy and it was arranged. It was not too surprising as the scholarship kids were working class and in our stratified society that was Scotland in the forties working class was always working class.

I had been given an excellent education at Lawside which gave me my love of Art and Classical Music. Mixing with "the cream of the crop" in our society I learned much from my classmates about confidence and leadership.

When I left school it did not take long to get an office job as "scholarship" kids were in great demand.

OUR NEW HOME

15

Our little home at 10 Mortimer Place was becoming crowded.
We were growing up, I at sixteen, Bette fourteen and Margaret
twelve, still shared a bed-room with brother David who was
now seven. It was not an easy situation and privacy was
impossible. We had been on the "housing list" for many years.
Remember that no new homes were built during our six years of
war.

Most of our city housing was in bad shape after the war (1945).
All of our government focus was on winning the war, there was
no time nor money for housing upkeep, which in many cases
was in much need of repair. The city council decided to tear
down the old and out-dated tenements and flats and build
modern apartments and semi-detached housing on the
outskirts of town.

At last!!!!!, when I was seventeen Dad got the keys to a council
house and we moved to a new semi-detached house in "St

Mary's Woods". Betty and I were now working and, with our wages adding to the family income, we were able to afford the extra rent

What a difference!!!!!! We had three bedrooms, a separate kitchen, a large living room and an indoor bathroom complete with bath.

Heating was still the open coal fire in the living room but there was a hot water heater behind the wall of the fireplace and we had hot water for household tasks and bathing. There was also a pipe that captured the hot air from the fireplace, and ran it upstairs. Before it vented outside it also ran through an airing cupboard in one of the bedrooms so we could hang our damp clothes to dry. The bedrooms had no heat so they were still freezing. Margaret and I shared one bedroom and bed (to keep us warm) and Bette shared the other bedroom with brother David. And Mum and Dad, at last had the privacy of their own bedroom.

Having an indoor bathroom and HOT running water was quite a luxury too, as was the kitchen complete with small boiler so we had no need to go out to wash clothes and our own drying green out back. And we could take a bath at home.

Still no central heating (this was 1947) so the coziest spot in the house was by the fire in the living room. Let me mention that the living room was a long room running the length of the house, with a window at each end. In winter time there was always ICE INSIDE THE WINDOWS at each side as the heat from the fire did not reach that far.......I think that all of us, huddling around the fireplace kept the heat focused on one place.....US.

I was really taken by the little door (like a doggie door) by the side of our front door....it was a little taller and wider than the size of a milk bottle, and that was it's purpose. Milkman slid the bottle and butter thru' the door, where, in the lobby, they did not freeze in the winter. I thought it was great.... all modern conveniences.

Mailman took the bus from town just like the rest of us and walked his route. Morning and afternoon on week-days and mornings on Saturday. He was like family, often I quickened my steps at lunchtime after meeting him at the bus stop, as he told me "You got a letter from him waiting". My boyfriend was in the army then so letters were something to look forward to.

We were so happy with our new house, the only drawback was that it was at the edge of town, which meant a twenty minute bus ride to get to the downtown shopping centers and movies and such. As nobody we knew had telephones it was impossible to communicate unless you were standing with a person. I remember coming home from work late one Friday, tired, ready for my tea, and reading good book by the fire. Found out that Betty had a bad case of 'flu and had been in bed all day. Problem was that she had a first date with a boy she REALLY LIKED. Thinking of him standing in the cold, wet weather and thinking he had been "stood up", he would never ask her out again. She pleaded with me to go explain to him, and what else could I do? Betty was my sister and she would have helped me. I reached for the damp coat I had just hung up, out into the cold, wet night, waited for the first bus into town. Transferred to the tram (they were meeting at Samuels downtown, which was next to the tram stop) Yes, there he was, looking miserable and I'm sure was getting ready to leave. After I explained, he brightened up considerably and yes, she did get her date another time. It was time consuming to live so far out but we sure loved our house.

We had a little fenced garden back and front, grandpa gave us all the starts for veggies and flowers and we had many strong backs in the family, so our house was lovely in a short time.

THE OFFICE

16

I started working in the office of an Ironmongers store a few months after leaving school. I had no idea of the business world or the working of an office, but I was smart, adaptable, a quick learner and, being a scholarship kid from one of the academies had already proven myself.

George Stephen and son was a well established Ironmonger and Steel business founded in my home town of Dundee in the year eighteen fourteen. My position was one of "office girl" (read go-fer) and was to learn the business from the ground up, all for the princely salary of eighteen shillings a week (about 20 dollars). It was a good starting wage for 1945, Dad was making about 35 dollars a week as an oiler in the jute mills at that time, so I felt like I was making a contribution to the family. I also was given an opportunity to advance to a little higher level than my other friends at home who worked on their feet all day in the jute mills or serving in the shops.

Hours were nine A.M. to six P.M. five days a week and eight A.M. 'til noon on Saturdays. There was an hour and a half break mid-day. In Scotland, this was our main meal and the large break gave you time to go home for dinner. The Ironmonger stores were not glorified hardware stores. We supplied farmers from all over Scotland with all kinds of essentials from lamps to tractors, also huge quantities of oil for said lamps, tractors, and all types of machinery. Our four salesmen travelled the length of Scotland to take orders for all that was needed and sell new gadgets as they became available.

Farmers in those days were quite a prosperous bunch many of them landed gentry befitting the title of Esquire (it was most important to address them by their title on any invoice or correspondence) These farms had done business with our firm for many generations and the correct protocol was observed. Tuesday was farmer's day and our town square was filled with farmers as they compared crops, bought and sold livestock and discussed the merits of their herds of cattle, sheep, etc. Our store was near the city square and on Tuesday was always filled with farmers.

We also supplied small factories in the nearby towns and villages with tools and other supplies. It was still a man's world in those days and all store personnel were men and "we girls" all seven of us (some having been with the firm all of their lives and were now in their fifties) ran the office under the orders of our owner and one manager.

I, being the office girl, sat across a large double desk from Mr Stephen, (I would guess he was about the third generation of his family to own and run the business) who was in his late sixties.

He sat next to the small coal fire, with his lifetime secretary in a small alcove nearby with her huge Underwood typewriter. I don't know where she had the strength to pound those heavy keys. The men in the shop made sure that the fire was always supplied but I think that the boss was the only one who got any heat from it. We had no heating or air conditioning in 1945, that was not the hardship it would seem, as there was no such thing as central heating in those days and we Scots were used to the cold.

I kept written records of orders etc. in ink (no ball point pens then, we used nibs and ink wells) in a ledger about a fifth my size. It held records of our yearly business. A storage room in our warehouse held similar ledgers covering one hundred and thirty years. It was so interesting to browse through the early records. The way of doing business had changed little and was all recorded in beautiful, flowery handwriting, penmanship was surely an art in earlier times. I was a messenger between our store and warehouse which was about one block away. I was entrusted with envelopes holding invoices and money to pay small bills in the nearby shops. Also ran all kinds of errands for the boss - stood in queues for fresh fish (In wartime there were queues everywhere). Got the daily newspaper from the vendor on the corner (who called me "smiler"). Also one pound of good coffee from the store up the street twice a week.

Of course, being the new girl in the office. I was a source of enjoyment to the men in the store. The shop manager sent me out one day to an industrial shop in town. "Anna, we are held up in one job because we don't have the right weight measure so I want you to go to xxxxx company and collect it for us. I have already phoned them so they know what we need". When I arrived there I told them I was from the ironmongers. The two gentlemen at the counter looked at each other and one said "you are lucky, this is the last long weight we have in stock" and off he goes to get it. I stood at the counter for some time and was beginning to worry that I wouldn't get back to the office before closing time. After an interminable time the man returned and said "You can go back to the store now, I think you have waited long enough". Of course, the men were laughing hysterically when I got back and I felt like a fool.

Our office phone was an old fashioned wall phone (this was in the forties), and, with me being so small, a box was placed there for me as I was occasionally allowed to take phone orders that came in. I had been there for about a week when one of the 'girls' said " Anna, will you please take this order from Arbroath Ironworks". I was so pleased with myself and felt quite grown up. We had no phones at home and using the phone was new to me. "Hello", I said, in my most grown up voice, "George Stephen and son ,may I take your order?" "Yes", the man replied, "I would like six dozen eight inch bastard files" My face went red at the mention of a cuss word (it was a word young ladies did not use in those days) and I did not know then that files came in smooth or bastard. What to do??? I went into the store and went to the manager. "I have an order for six dozen files" "O.K." said Mr Beattie, "what kind" "eight inches" said I. "But what kind?" he says "I don't know" I replied " well, you had better get back to the phone and take the complete order" As I returned to the office, he called to the men in the store "Anna just got an order for files" They well knew what he was talking about and gathered near. I went back to the phone and stood there for a minute, I knew the man's order, but I was a good Catholic girl who would never utter a cuss word. What could I do?..... I didn't want to lose my job. So I went back to the shop. "Well?" said Mr Beattie..... He wants xxxxx files I said in a whisper. The men were all standing around listening.

"WHAT?" said Mr Beattie. "xxxxxx files I said. "You'll have to speak up.... you can't keep a man on the phone all day 'til we know if we can supply his order". It was now or never "B-A-S-T-A-R-D files" I said as loud as I could, my face as red as fire. "That's better" said Mr Beattie, "Tell the customer that we will have his order out this afternoon" I escaped to the office and remembered to tell the priest at my next confession that I had said a swear word.

I was so very naive and the men were just having some fun. Remember that it was the forties and there was no TV so young office girls were the source of much amusement.

While working at the ironmongers the boss's secretary, Annie, had found out that I was a Gold Medalist in song. She mentioned a competition to me one day, but I wasn't interested. I was timid and shy in many ways and had never done any singing except at home or with the support of my school. Mom and Dad were quiet and humble folk who would never have encouraged me in such a venture. So that was the end of the matter....... so I thought.

A few days later Annie came and put something on my desk. It was a piece of sheet- music. "There" she said, "I entered you in the competition". What was I to do? It had already been arranged and Annie had bought the music. The song was from a new movie musical in 1945. Promoting the movie, the songs were heard frequently on the radio which was the only means of advertising in sound. A further promotion in each town was a competition featuring the movie songs and members of the community. This was held on the first night the movie was shown, so there was an added interest in going to "the pictures" that night. As I had turned sixteen I was just old enough to compete in the open competition. The song Annie had chosen for me from the songs in the musical was "I'll be your sweetheart" which was also the title of the movie.

The heavy promotion of the songs by radio worked in my favor as soon everyone was singing or whistling the tunes. Lucky for me, as I had no piano at home and no music teacher to show me how to engage an audience or learn the melody.

Don't remember the first audition but I ended up being one of five chosen to compete on "opening" night. This was done during intermission. The lights went up and it was announced that two winners would be chosen from audience applause. After each singing our chosen song, lights went down and we were lined up across the stage about five feet apart. I was at the last place at the left side of the stage. Dimmer lights showed the singers but the audience was dark. A spotlight shone on the first Contestant to so-so applause, then to the second one...... thunderous applause..... it was obvious that she was the winner. The spotlight then turned to the third one, but, instead of applause, there was a voice from the audience. "No, No, it's the wee lassie" Right away there was a chorus of voices calling "the wee lassie" and the spotlight swung directly on to me......I was nearly blinded and scared to death but the applause left no doubt and I was awarded second prize. How about that??? The money prize was nice and I bought a new pair of shoes with it.....but I had no illusions of becoming a singer. I loved to sing but that was as far as it went. I was glad the competition was over and that Annie was pleased with me.

FIRST DATE

17

My work at the ironmongers kept me busy. Monday thru' Friday 9 A.M. TO 6 P.M. and Saturday 'til noon. I also had my chores at home and my spare time found me sitting by the fire reading. (I loved books and all kinds of stories - when I was much younger "Grimms Fairy Tales" was a favorite of mine, also loved poetry)

One night, as I was sitting by the fire reading, as usual, a cousin about my age came by on an errand for her mom. I looked up from my book, said "hello" and went back to my reading. "you are all dressed up, where are you off to?" my mum asked my cousin Ina. "I'm off to the dancin'" said Ina. "I wish you would take Anna next time and get her out of the house" said Mum. So next time Ina went to "the dancin'" I went along and so began another stage in my life.

We went to a small dance hall called "Robinsons"on the other side of town. "The dancin'" was a very respectable place in those days - it was a way for young folks to pass the evenings.

Television was unheard of and BBC went off the air at 9 P.M. We young folks had two forms of entertainment "the pictures" or "the dancin".

Robinsons did not have a band, but played "Victor Sylvester" dance music. The good things about the place .... no alcoholic beverages and no one allowed who was over nineteen. It was open from 7 P.M. to 10 P.M. Monday, Wednesday and Friday. Ina and I went on Fridays. Robinsons was the only teen spot in town and we saw many kids we had gone to school with. As at school the boys and girls were always kept separate, we all seemed to follow the same rule at the dancin'

The guys stood at one side of the dance hall. The music would start and they would have to walk quite a distance to the girls. We watched the guys walk over but they usually danced with the regulars they had danced with before. Ina and I, being new, danced all our dances together. In fact there were many girls dancing together. If a waltz or a two-step was played it was all girls dancing - too much footwork for the guys.

After Ina and I either danced together (always aware that the guys were checking us out) or were "wallflowers" maybe about three weeks, a young man came over and asked me to dance. Don't remember much about my first dance with a boy. It sure wasn't like we saw in the movies – glamorous couple gazing into each other's eyes and floating on a cloud. We didn't look at each other and we didn't make easy conversation - the fact of the matter is that neither of us could dance very well so most of our conversation was "SORRY" as we each took turns at treading on each other's toes. It couldn't have been too bad as he came back for more punishment...oops, I mean dancing the next week. I thought that he was too old for me as he was nineteen and I had just become seventeen, but he was a very polite young man and seemed to like me. It was flattering to receive such grown-up attention.

Found out that his name was Frank, after being apprentice in his trade for four years, he had just become a journeyman carpenter at Caledonian shipyard in town. Originally from Glasgow he had come to live with relatives in Dundee when his parents died. He never mentioned his parents again but I got the idea that he was not too happy living with relatives.

After a month steady on Friday nights Ina and I became "regulars" and so were dancing more with the guys. Still on slow nights I could always count on my original partner for a few dances.

After three Fridays of dancing together, Frank finally came over for the "last dance". In our dancing tradition that meant only one thing. Frank was going to ask to walk me home. He must have been so unsure of himself, it took him almost the whole dance before he had the courage to ask. I could have turned him down....but I didn't. It seemed strange walking with a young man instead of my girlfriends or cousin. After three weeks of walking me home Frank got a good-night kiss. This was real serious business.....then he started to phone me at work. This was not as easy as it would seem as Frank had no access to a phone in the shipyard and spent most of his lunch time walking almost a mile to the nearest phone booth where he would wait, most times in terrible weather (Scotland is not known for dry, sunny days) If the booth was occupied, he had to wait, sometimes he didn't get to use the phone at all as he couldn't be late back to work.

About five weeks after that first dance, Frank asked if I would like to go to the pictures (movies) with him and I agreed. No, he didn't pick me up at home. We had two modes of transportation in town...... bus or tram car. I met him at Samuels store downtown which was the usual meeting place for dates, convenient as it was next to the tram stop. From there we walked a couple of blocks to the theatre where we joined the queue for the second showing of the movie, about seven-o-clock.

Saturday was always date night for many reasons. No work next day - you could stay out 'til ten or eleven at night. For me, as work at the office was finished at noon I had many hours to prepare. All expenses were taken care of by the dater (Frank) it was unheard of for a girl to pay her way, that was the privilege of the man. I chose the time and the movie, after all, if I didn't enjoy date one, there would be no date two. So first films were soppy, romantic "chick flicks". Musicals of the day were very popular (think Fred Astaire and Ginger Rogers). After a date I got to chose if the boy got a good-night kiss. GIRLS RULE!!!! At least on first dates.

Watching the clock at work, I was ready to go exactly at noon. As office girl one of my first duties was the office mail so my first stop was at the Post Office. From there to the bus stop to wait impatiently for a number five bus (or was it seven?) to St Mary's Woods. Buses were so busy as most folks were downtown on Saturdays.

Lucky for me! I was far up in the queue and got on the first bus available. Then there was the walk to the house, where Mum had the dinner ready. Saturday and Sunday dinners were leisurely family affairs. There was no gulp and run at our house. Surely, Mum did not understand the importance of first dates.

We were not allowed to date 'til age sixteen, so my siblings did not make things easy for me, never knowing the nervousness of first dates themselves. "Will you get out of the bathroom. I have to have a bath" I say in a slightly loud voice. Fifteen minutes later I appeal to Mum. "Come on now, stop teasing your sister, she has a date tonight" says Mum. A couple of minutes later Margaret opens the door. "Who has a bath at three in the afternoon? Anna wants to smell good for her boyfriend HA! HA!" says Margaret. Never any sympathy from siblings.

After bathing I get to the serious stuff - hair wash –it will take ages to dry. No electric hair driers, this was to be a natural process. With hair drying I could now think of what to wear..why didn't I think of that ahead of time? (but I never did). Luckily, or unluckily I did not have a wardrobe full of clothes so the selection did not take long. Then ironing blouse or dress or press skirt. Why didn't I do this ahead of time? (but I never did). Get moving....heat iron on stove- towels on dining table, a little work and I soon have something to wear. What time is it now???? O.K. Find clean stockings with no runs in them. Then polish shoes......GOOD!! Hair still drying. Sit for fifteen minutes by the fire and fluff my hair to help it dry. Can read a magazine at the same time, helps me to relax.

Of course, this did not happen in a vacuum. It was Saturday and relatives would pop in from time to time. "Anna" my mum said "there's the bakery van, go get a cake for tea-time" "I can't, Mum, my hair isn't dry yet" "Well, Bette, you go" says mum. "You asked Anna first" Bette said. "Well, I'm asking you now" mum insisted. "Just because she has a date I have to do everything" Bette was mad. "You're just jealous" says I. Bette was not yet of dating age. There was always much energy in a house with teenagers and we had three teen girls.

Had my tea early, at four-thirty. Quarter of an hour later I was ready for make-up and hair curling. It was a tricky business, this hair curling using curling tongs heated on the stove. We tested it with wet fingers and the trick was getting the tongs at the right heat. Not hot enough and hair stayed flat, too hot and it was frizz. Too, too hot and you burned your fingers. We had practiced this for family occasions and became quite adept at judging. Of course being first date nervous I had to be extra careful.

I was ten minutes late for my date. Not unusual as I had to transfer from bus to the tram which stopped at our meeting place. Trying to make conversation with Frank as we walked to the movie theatre I said "Did you have a good day?" "Oh aye!" said Frank "went to a football (soccer) match with my buddies this afternoon. Great Game. Dundee won" If he had only known how I spent my afternoon. I was soon dating others but Frank was still dating me too and dating me more often and after a few months we were "going steady". It wasn't really serious but I was going out with Frank once a week, and we weren't dating others so I guess we were going steady.

We had been to the movies one Saturday to see a musical. Everything seemed as normal....it was a good movie, Frank walked me home, said "Good night, I'll try to call you on Monday" I didn't receive a call on Monday but, thought nothing of it as that wasn't unusual. Boss possibly kept him busy, or he had an impromptu game of soccer on the dinner hour.

However, I was having my "tea" after work on Monday..Knock on door. Dad answered it and came back to me. "It's Frank's aunt asking for you" he said. Mystified, I had never met the woman. "Hi" I said. Her question "were you out with Frank on Saturday?" "Yes" I replied. "Did he say anything to you about leaving?" she said. I was confused "I don't know what you are talking about" I said. "Frank left for your date on Saturday and didn't come home. We havn't heard from him, his friends don't know where he is and I think he may have told you" The woman was very worried but I couldn't help her.

The letter I received four days later explained the mystery. Frank had joined the Army and was training at barracks in Perth. When training was finished he was assigned to the tank corps. Whether by his request or not I never knew. It led him on a journey I'm sure he could not imagine. We are talking about 1947 and the world was at peace.

Frank was assigned to a Tank Division in England. I saw him a couple of times when he was home on leave, and we wrote occasionally but no more dancing every week and few dates. We had dated for only a few months, gradually the letters stopped and I dated others. (I was just seventeen). I saw Frank a couple of times after that, usually when I was out with my boyfriend and he was seeing a young woman in Dundee.

I went on with my life and he with his and I didn't see or hear of him 'til 1953. I was married and was soon to emigrate to Canada. Upon meeting a friend of his downtown he asked "Did you hear about Frank?" I replied " I havn't heard of him in years, How is he?" "Bad news" said his friend "He died in a P.O.W. camp in North Korea"

We sometimes make decisions when we are young, which lead to tragic conclusions. Frank was a really nice young man and I was privileged to have known him.

SINGING

18

In 1938 our family was growing and Dad had been looking for a better paying job with some chance of promotion. He started with the Dundee Transportation department. First as a cleaner, keeping the tramcars and buses spotless and shiny, but, being a smart and responsible employee, he soon became a streetcar conductor and then a driver.

He looked so smart in his uniform and we were so proud of him. Sometimes, in the early evenings of summer, Mum would take us downtown and we would transfer to Dad's tram and ride the route to the end of his shift which was on the edge of Dundee (a place called Lochee). There he would treat us to ice cream at a little Italian shop that had the best ice cream in town. In those days the product was made on site in small batches and the results were individual and delicious.

We were so proud to be driven by our Dad you would think that the tramcar was personally ours. We were always on our best behavior and those evenings were a real special time.

Dad's conductor in 1946 was a man called Bob Nelson. Together every day, they soon became good friends, Mum also became friends with his wife. Although Bob was Dad's conductor, his circumstances were different from ours. They lived in a nice council house and even had their own car. Something unusual in those days.

Mrs Nelson was Belgian, had grown up in Brussels and had gone to a private Art School there. She was an artist in design and color. They had three sons, one was an Air Force pilot who went missing in a raid over Germany at the beginning of World War II and was listed as "missing in action" presumed killed. They never heard of him again so he had died in action. He was never mentioned although I'm sure he was sadly missed for a lifetime.

The two other sons had graduated from University - one was an art teacher, the other an optometrist. Who would guess that this family would have me furthering my love of music? The boys had a Scottish Country Dance Band - one played drums and the other directed and also played fiddle. They performed at various dances and functions in the area. Well known and well liked, they had just decided to start a "concert party". In addition to the Band, they had a classical, solo violinist, a country dance team, a comedian, and needed a singer to complete the group.

In conversation one day, Mrs Nelson mentioned the concert party endeavor to Mum. "Anna won the silver and gold medals in Scots Folk Songs" said Mum. The boys were interested so I was taken over to sing for them one day. They were quite impressed with my singing.....the fact that I was seventeen and quite easy on the eyes didn't hurt either. They had a friend who could be my piano accompanist, so just like that, the party was complete. In addition to my office work, I now had rehearsals, and concerts around town.

"Where does Anna study" asked Mrs Nelson one day. Mum was surprised "Anna never had any lessons" she replied. "Oh, she has a lovely voice, she must study further" said Mrs Nelson. My parents had never thought of voice lessons but, at her insistence, they enrolled me in "Dundee School of Music" and so I was introduced to serious classical performance. I don't know how they managed to pay for lessons, but they did, and I will be forever grateful.

We had no piano and practicing was difficult in our little apartment, so my practicing was limited to my one lesson a week. But I was singing, learning how to use my voice, work with an accompanist and know the protocol for the concert stage. I was also invited to join the "School of Music" choir (quite an honour) where we concertized around town and also did some broadcasts for BBC in Edinburgh.

The concert party was not yet performance ready. Under the direction of our comedian we were all involved in "blackout skits" which helped to round out our show.

Mrs Nelson, meantime, was making dresses for our four country dance ladies. Long, white, ankle length dresses, worn with a tartan sash over the shoulder and across the bodice, caught with a "cairngorm" Scottish broach at the shoulder. Long, white gloves and soft leather "gillie slippers" (something like ballet slippers) which laced up the ankles.

The four men in the team wore kilts, in tartans of their own choosing, with sporran and traditional Sgian dubh (small single edged knife in the tops of their stockings, Scotland in Olden Times was a dangerous place. Most Scotsmen in those days spent much time in the heathered hills... hunting food or fighting enemies, either Englishmen or other Clansmen and these daggers hidden in their stockings served for defense or as eating utensils). Men of our dance team wore white dress shirts, highland jacket, tartan tie matching their kilts and also wore "Gillie slippers". Scots Country Dancing is formal and graceful and our dancers made quite an impression on stage.

You would think that with me being a Scottish Song medalist I would be singing Scottish Songs but that was not so. We had the dance band and dance team, so we needed something of a variety. I had a high soprano voice, known as coloratura and my music teachers had been stressing this uniqueness. The high notes, trills and runs impressed the audience and at that time this type of singing was popular. Think Deanna Durbin, Anna Maria Alberghetti and Jane Powell. This is the kind of music which I sang.

I remember my formal dress for the first big performance of our concert party. Mrs Nelson, with her artist's eye, knew exactly what to make for me. Fitting bodice and white, full, but not too full skirt. Bodice was white, with a shawl collar, The center, focal part of the bodice was imprinted with large, beautiful flowers, in blue, pink and purple, it looked like a painting. Then she used an overlay of fine white tulle over the skirt. Around this overlay, from bodice to hemline were six bands of velvet ribbon, in blue, pink and purple, about one and a half inches wide, and about three and a half inches apart, matching the flowers on the bodice. Mrs Nelson never used patterns and this was all her own design. It was the most beautiful evening dress I ever owned. Long, white, over the elbow gloves and white slippers completed the picture.

The whole show was classical and lovely, as were the concerts in those days. Too bad we couldn't have a color video but this was 1947 and we didn't have recording equipment like we do today.

First big concert was in the tourist town of Carnoustie and was well received. I was to sing only one number, a French coloratura song called "Villanelle" and the audience really approved. Towards the end of the concert, the announcer asked if I had anything else I could sing. I was taught at music school to always have an encore on hand, knowing that, the announcer went on stage, "During intermission I had many people tell me how they enjoyed our singer. Do you think you can persuade her to sing again?" much applause...He called out to me (of course I was already in the wings). I came onstage to much applause and answered "yes"......I sang "Songs My Mother Taught Me" (the music already on the piano) and brought the house down. The audience thought this was all their own doing but it had been nicely set up.

After the concert, I mentioned to the announcer my surprise people asking for an encore. His reply, "Oh, nobody did, but we knew you had the audience and it was a good chance to get you back on stage".

So I learned another lesson about gauging an audience. I had so much to learn about stage work. The concert party lasted a little over two years, we performed at little tourist towns in summer, at company business affairs, churches and hospitals, one memorable one at Ashludi, our hospital for TB patients who had been quarantined. However, everyone had full time day jobs and, although we all enjoyed and loved "show business", it fell to the boys to take care of all the arrangements, phoning and rehearsals, while still performing themselves and it became too much for them. We had great fun reacting with the audience and sharing our talents with others but the work-a-day world could not be denied.

I was still taking voice lessons and singing with the "school of Music" choir. Some of the choir belonged to the Dundee Opera Company and persuaded me to audition. I duly sang for the judges and became a member.

The Society was started in 1872 as "The Dundee Amateur Opera" it was disbanded in 1892, and was revived as "Dundee Operatic Society" in 1902 and is still going strong today (2012), although the musical presentations have changed "dramatically" to suit the new age.

We started rehearsals in September of the year with two weeks of performance in February or March of the following year. The first year I was a member I was asked to join the dancing team in addition to my chorus work. Seems that the team lost a dancer when she relocated to England and our choreographer thought I could fill her place. There were eight members of the dance team and it was great fun. We did some great numbers in

"Rose Marie" and "The Belle of New York". Including a wild Can Can, although sedate enough for the time and culture.

The company, at that time did an Opera and a Musical each year. In 1952 we performed "The Bohemian Girl" by Balfe and "The Belle of New York" by Kerker. 1953 we performed "Martha" by von Flotow and "Rose Marie" by Friml

In 1954 I emigrated to Canada but I really missed "Dundee Operatic Society" and the joy of singing with them. Would I be able to continue with my music in Canada? I had no idea what lay ahead.

DATING TWO

19

After Frank and I had parted company I had the usual Saturday night dates, many times in a group with my girlfriends and their dates. Nothing serious, as I was busy with my singing and my work. Music and singing was still my joy. Not many, in fact not any of the young men I dated cared about classical music. I didn't care for partying and "football" and I was enjoying my dancing at the Opera Company.

I was spending much time with the 'School of Music" choir and we had many bus trips to concerts out of town and did some BBC concerts from Edinburgh. It was great fun but no guys as it was a "Young Ladies Choir". Our director was the only male and I don't know how he put up with a bus load full of chattering females. His favorite plea was "Ladies, Ladies , don't talk so much......save your voices for the performance". It didn't work very well when he was outnumbered thirty to one.......
Wonderful director that he was, he only had authority during rehearsals and concerts.

At work I had learned much in my two years at George Stephen and Son, had moved to a position in accounting and decided to move on to a company called DPM (Dundee Pasteurized Milk) and worked in their main office.

It was a huge company which included labs for the testing of the milk... horses and stables and carts for the delivery of milk..... and many restaurants and bakeries in town. This was a very complex operation. Big vans picked up milk from the nearby farms. First step was the pasteurization.... Then testing the product in the lab of the before they were sent out to the stores and individual customers.

There was also the transportation for all this. We had our own fleet of vans. While I was employed there (around 1948) our electric vans were introduced replacing the horse drawn carts. These small vans did not look different from all the others on the road. It was their noise, or lack of it that was so different. Movement on our roads was usually accompanied by "clip-clop" or "vroom". These vans just made a small humming noise. They did not move very fast, come to think of it though, they were just as fast as the old horse drawn milk carts and the company did not have the upkeep of stables, vets, blacksmiths, feeds, etc. I worked in the purchasing department and it was very interesting work though the pay could have been better.

Things were changing at home. My two sisters now had steady boyfriends. Betty was going out with a young airman from Leuchars Air Force Base, Margaret had been dating Jack since she was sixteen and me????.......I was still busy with my music, had occasional dates, but no one special.

Our youngest sister, Margaret, was the first to marry. She and Jack started dating when she was sixteen and Jack was eighteen. They had never dated anyone else, their song was "They tried to tell us we're too young". Jack was a first class football (soccer) player and signed for our home team Dundee United a second division team when he turned eighteen. After one and a half years, he had made quite a name for himself and decided to move to a first division team in Glasgow. After signing a contract with them and with what looked like a good future ahead he and Margaret decided to set a wedding date. They married in December 1952….. Margaret was just over eighteen and Jack was twenty.

With Margaret leaving home on her marriage we were going to be one paycheck short . In those days family stayed at home until marriage and most of their wages went to the household. You were never in charge of your paycheck 'til you were married and setting up your own home.

I was ready to move on, and this was a good time to look for a better paying work. I started in charge of inventory control in a Dundee firm which made circular looms for sale to India, which by now was processing it's own jute products.

We were now living in our council house on the edge of town, and it took the best part of an hour to get to work. There was about a one mile walk to the bus stop located at Blackshades, a community closer to town. Built before our houses they were known as " the prefabs"..

Waiting at the bus stop at seven-thirty each morning I noticed a young man about my age, who used the same bus stops that I did.

After a few weeks introduction to my new employment at their main office, I was shown to my office, which was on it's own upstairs by the supply office which was outside the shop where technicians made the looms.

My office had the records book for the assemblies and sub-assemblies with their code numbers . I would get requisitions from the floor manager for a number of assemblies or sub-assemblies to be built. Records showed the parts for the assembly (nuts, bolts, rods etc.) and size needed for each part . Multiplying this by the number of looms being built, I would make up the order for supplies to be delivered to the shop. Shop manager would give me his signature for "parts received" which I, in turn, deducted from my inventory records and ordered new parts, as needed to keep supplies available. It was a responsible and very interesting job.

After I was settled in (about a couple of weeks) a technician came into my office to check on the status of a "shop order"........Who would it be, but the young man from my bus stop. I found out later that he had persuaded his manager that he be the liaison between shop and office, so saw him quite a lot. Of course, I couldn't ignore him at the bus stop so we shared a seat on the bus five days a week. And, obviously, on a half hour journey, we talked, first about the job and the weather. Then a little about ourselves.

Norman was two years older than me. He lived in Blackshades with his Mother (Irish) and Scottish father and had two sisters. Father had lived most of his life in Dundee and as a young man had immigrated to Toronto in Canada.

Many people from Britain and Ireland re-located to Toronto in the mid- nineteen twenties, where jobs were plentiful and wages excellent. A good number were young and single and, meeting with others of much the same heritage, they fell in love, married and had children. New citizens in Canada, they started their new life, set down roots and did very well....until "The Depression" started to take it's toll and jobs disappeared. Such a difficult time for emigrants, who, for the most part, did not have the protection of extended families. Married couples with children to feed and support were reluctantly forced to spend their last dollars on a boat trip home to stay with family. Life was difficult during "The Depression" years but many who had to leave still had dreams of one day returning to the opportunities they had seen existed in "The New World" for them and their children. Norman was born in Toronto and was a Canadian citizen although he had lived in Scotland since he was three years old.

It became a routine thing, we rode the bus together just two employees of the same firm. After leaving the bus we went our separate ways. I to the front entrance where I clocked-in at the office and he to the worker's entrance where he clocked-in with the technicians, apprentices and service and foundry workers (the company also made many of it's own parts – hence the foundry). I would say the company was 96 percent male the only women being office staff and kitchen where we had our own canteen. Even there the office staff had their own private room. During the day there was a strict line between the office staff and others and everything was on a purely business level.

Eventually, someone noticed Norman and I leaving the bus together and Norman was finding more excuses during the day to confer with me in my office. Soon they were teasing him mercilessly and after a while (unknown to me) were taking bets on how soon he would ask me out.

We rarely caught the same bus home after work as we had our own social lives. However, one Friday, there he was at the bus stop. "Got plans with your boyfriend this week-end?" he asked after we were seated. "Going dancing with my girlfriends" I said "Don't have a steady boyfriend"

One morning a week later he said "Have you seen that picture at the "Playhouse". "No" says I " but I hear it is great" "How about if we see it together?" said he. It was still a platonic relationship on my part but we went out and enjoyed each other's company.

Norman was different from the other young men I had dated. We came from the same kind of background, although his Mum and Dad spent the early part of their marriage in Canada. What made him different was that he was a lead drummer of our drum corps in the Dundee Scottish Pipe Band. This took talent and dedication.

He took part in many concerts and parades, we were alike in many ways and had the same disciplines in our talents. With my singing I stood alone in competition and concert to be judged by my peers and audience. Norman as part of a large group still had solo work. We both had the nervousness of wanting to do our best in performance. And, of course, there was the daily practice and weekly rehearsals. We caught the same bus on Wednesday evenings, he leaving at Dudhope Castle for Band while I continued to town for Opera rehearsals.

Pipe Band parades were in full Highland regalia complete with bearskin hats, white spats and traditional kilts. Uniforms had to be perfect as had marching and music. There were many competitions such as the one held in Glasgow each year as the bands vied for the World Championship. There were also parades and the massed bands on special occasions. The most famous being the Braemar Highland Games each year with the Royal Family in attendance. Queen Elizabeth 11 stays close to her Scottish heritage.

Full Highland regalia is not worn at competitions. Remember that the Pipes and Drums were a military unit used on the battlefield. In the early 16th century each company of infantry soldiers would be led into battle by a single drummer and fife player. The drums were for signals, not music, staying close to the company commander to convey orders, as a shouted command could not be heard in the heat of battle. In later years the bugle took over from the drum.

In competition they were judged as a military unit. They wore stout shoes with silver buckles and kilts. The bearskin hat was replaced by a Glengarry bonnet. This was a fitted cap made of heavy wool with the traditional red toorie on top of the military insignia on the side. There were four judges who had been players themselves and had to pass a rigorous test to get their certificate. Two for pipes, one for drums and one for dress, military marching and formation. They were judged on clarity of tone for pipes, crispness and complexity of pattern for the drum corps, clean changes of tempo for all and, as a military unit, uniform and marching.

We were both busy, me with singing and he with band but we did see each other every week day at work and had bus journeys together. He and his two pals came to see the Opera's production of "Rose Marie" (not quite soccer but they seemed to enjoy it). I went with the band to some of the highland games, where, when Norman was busy with band, I had the company of the girls who were going out with band members and, before we knew it, we were going steady.

I met his family and he met mine so we were together at all the family activities. Six months later Norman proposed and I accepted. We were married in July 1953.

Our wedding was a big family affair, mostly mine as Norman did not have many family in town. But between the two of us we had many friends from our various associations and schools. Being a member of the choir, they all turned out to sing at the ceremony, as did my music teacher, who was a very fine tenor soloist. The band from the concert party played for the dancing at the reception.

My two sisters were bridesmaids and two adorable daughters of cousins were flower girls. The flower girls, both aged four, were so good and responsible in the roles (I found out soon enough that they had been bribed as, at the most solemn part of the ceremony, one turned from her place by the bridesmaids to call to her mother "when do I get my Jello?"). Norman's best friends from childhood, Bill and Andy, were groomsmen, while my young brother, then aged fourteen assisted the ushers.

It was a lovely wedding and we honeymooned in the resort town of Oban in Argyll, which is fifty miles North-West of Glasgow in a beautiful area close to Loch Lomond and the Trossachs National Park.

MARRIAGE- FIRST YEAR

20

We had been busy planning a wedding and finding a place to live. There were no apartments available.......our city housing was in a shambles as we went through the war years, no repairs were done on all the old buildings, many one hundred years old and older with cold running water, no bathrooms and outside toilet. The city decided that is would be better and cheaper to demolish and re-build rather than try to renovate.

This destroying and re-building was a slow process and there was a long list of potential renters. Of course, older folks with families had first preference while newly weds were at the bottom of the list so it looked like we could wait a year or two for a place of our own.

The lucky people were the ones already renting council houses from the city. These had been built about ten or fifteen years before the war and had two or three bedrooms, living room, kitchen and indoor bathroom. After the war years many retirees living in these houses rented out a bedroom to help with their living expenses. This was not allowed but the city pretended not to notice as there was such a dire need for housing.

So Norman and I checked the newspapers and started on our round of council houses. We had luck at the first one we tried. The widow who lived there had seen "Rose Marie" recently and remembered me from the Opera. That's the beauty of being in the dancing chorus. There were only eight of us and we had center stage on many occasions. So, when we returned from our honeymoon we moved into a furnished room at Mrs Brown's. She had two rooms for rent and the other was already taken by a quiet young man who had the bedroom next to ours. Not quite the thing for a young married couple but we were lucky to rent a place with an indoor bathroom.

Our little room had a fireplace for heating which made it cozy. We had a little table and a few chairs , ate all our meals in our combined bedroom-living room-dining room so we had privacy in our everyday living. Thank goodness we also had use of the kitchen to prepare our meals, we could even have a couple of friends or family to share a meal occasionally

Most of our lives we had lived in crowded conditions so this was no hardship. We were a young couple in love. We were both working and between us brought in a nice salary- even had a savings account. We were still looking for our own place. In fact, with a positive attitude, we had just bought some living room furniture from a store in town. Did I say bought?? This was a good sale and we were able to put a down payment on the furniture of our choice. Part of our salary each month went towards the furniture which should not be ours 'til paid in full in a little over one year. We figured by that time we might have our own little place, Hope springs eternal, and our ongoing purchase reminded us that our one room rental was short term.

Grandma and Grandpa Clark had the first invitation to a Sunday dinner. Mrs Brown was such a kind landlady. She cleared out the kitchen for me, but stayed nearby to answer any questions I had about roast beef and roasted potatoes, even asked my permission (gladly given) to help prepare the veggies. Everything went well except the rice pudding for dessert when I used to much raw rice. Luckily she noticed in time and we just started over again.

Grandma and Grandpa were duly impressed by my first dinner. Our little room was lovely. Most of our wedding gifts were stored at Mums but I kept out a lovely china tea set and crystal glasses . Also some linen wear and tablecloths, some of which I had embroidered and had in my "hope chest" before I was married. Bed had a beautiful blue/gray comforter, a gift from my Uncle John (he of the car and business). The table had a delicate blue cloth and colourful flowers in a crystal vase (another wedding gift)...I was really pleased with my little "home".

Norman still had the Pipe Band and I had my choir and music lessons, that, and the fact that we both worked, kept us busy and we were settling into married life.

About six months into our marriage, approximately January 1954, Norman began to speak about Canada , and then moving to Canada. That surprised me, I had no thought of leaving Scotland and my family. Only one cousin of mine (Grace) had moved abroad after she married an Australian Airman and emigrated as a war bride. My sister Margaret now lived in England where her husband Jack played football (soccer) but she visited Dundee often.

Come to think of it, one of Norman's sisters now lived in Toronto with her Canadian husband and little baby son. He also had an Aunt and Uncle who had not returned to Scotland during the Depression. The plan seemingly was for Norman and I to emigrate, then his Mum , Dad and sister would follow us. His parents had met and married in Toronto twenty years before and had always wanted to return.

There was not much I could do..... in the early fifties the husband made the decisions.

Now our whole focus shifted. Norman went downtown himself one Saturday to cancel our furniture. Luckily for him, the store refunded everything when they knew we were emigrating (very generous of them). So our furniture savings went into the fund for Canada. Boat fares, passports, we started sending our wedding gifts by steamer trunk care of Norman's sister. Many people were leaving Britain at this time and our Government bureaucracy was so slow. We had to travel to Glasgow a few times before they could start to process our passports, of course, Norman needed a Canadian passport so that slowed things further. Then we needed a Doctor's clean bill of health, then there were the necessary vaccinations. I was so sick from the Smallpox vaccination (which was mandatory) I still have the scar to this day.

We finally got all the papers in order and were given a sailing date in August. I had to notify the Opera I would not be back, remember, they would need time to replace one of their dancers, Music School, church choir and, of course, all of my friends and my friends from work. There were many tears at the going-away-party they threw for me. It was like I was dismantling my whole life. However, being Scottish I did what I had to do as I accompanied my husband to our new life in Canada.

OH!! CANADA????

21

So many people on the station platform and I loved them all. My family was here to see us off on our journey to the New World, otherwise known as Canada "There's the train" yelled my young cousin, as if anyone could miss the behemoth belching black smoke.

My heart gave a funny little lurch......was it fear or anticipation? Maybe a little of both. After all, I was only the second in my large extended family to leave our home town of Dundee, for another country. A cousin left for Australia as a war bride in 1946, nothing has changed since I immigrated and all of my family still live in Scotland now (2012).

The year was 1954 and I, at twenty- four , had never traveled from the land of my birth. I had been married for one year to Norman, born in Canada but living in Scotland since a baby. But he did have an uncle aunt and cousins in Canada and a sister who had emigrated one year before, with his parents and his other sister to follow us in one year. But for me, this was goodbye to the town I knew, people I loved, my music and the Operatic Society which nurtured my artistic ideals. Did they have Opera in Canada? I told myself "don't be silly Anna, you are not falling off the planet" Women of my generation were expected to defer to "the man 'o the hoose" and if his decision was to live in Canada that was it.

There was so much confusion and excitement as we boarded the train with our two suitcases holding our every day possessions. Most of our wedding gifts, china, cutlery, linens etc. had been sent by trunk to Norman's sister in Toronto. "Cheerio!" I said " I'll write as soon as I get there. "At that time phones were the luxury of the rich, not working folks like us. So writing was our only means of communication.

I scanned all the beloved faces, imprinting them on my heart, suddenly I couldn't make out the faces as the tears blotted out all else but my sorrow. The train was packed with no seats to be had, so, for a while discomfort took the place of sorrow, as we sat on suitcases in the train corridor for the eight hour journey to England. I'll always remember August the eighth as the date we arrived in Southhampton.I remembered it was Granma Clark's 78 birthday, so I had to send a card before we went to the ship. No such thing as stopping overnight at a hotel, working folks like us had no money for such luxuries. We were to go directly to the ship. Of course this never bothered us as that is the way it always had been.

Lugging our belongings onto the bus we finally arrived at the docks. IT WAS THE BIGGEST SHIP I HAD EVER SEEN. Now I know that lurching of the heart......it was fear....I was leaving the security of life within a large family for the unknown.

Three days journey by ship, I was sea sick, as were most of the passengers, most of the time. I shared a cabin with three other women. Norman and I could not afford a cabin where we could be together and all this made for a miserable journey.

Upon arriving in Canada, at Montreal I think, my first memories were of standing on deck, unbearably hot after the coolness of a Scottish summer. I was in a long queue of several hundred new emigrants waiting to go through immigration......I was alone.

My husband of one year, born in Canada had no need for immigration formalities and was eager to view his new country. I waited alone in the heat, amid strangers. Was this a portend of things to come?

The last leg of our journey was by train in the dark of night. I was so tired but could not rest. I remember being intrigued by all the little resorts we passed with all their little fairy lights. But it was so hot and humid.... I had not even imagined such heat at night..... 68 or 70 degrees was as hot as it got during the day in Scotland and here we were at night and the temperature must have been near eighty or ninety degrees. It seemed impossible that it was so hot and humid at nine o clock at night.

Sister in law and her husband met us and took us to a rental room in a large house. When they left I thought "now for a good sleep". As I was dozing off.....ZZZZ...what was that?.....ZZZZ... high pitched sound.....mosquitoes. Having arrived in Toronto at the height of the mosquito season.....and being from a cool climate...we opened the windows to let the cool night air in....BIG MISTAKE!. Finally, too exhausted to care about insects.. I fell asleep.

Awakened next morning, Sunday, by the sound of church bells. Toronto, with it's many churches was a cacophony of bells on Sunday morning. It reminded me of the church bells in Dundee......I was homesick already.

TORONTO

22

Work in Toronto in 1954 was plentiful and we found employment in short order. Norman as a purchasing agent in an engineering firm and me an inventory control position in Pitney-Bowes of Canada.

Norman's sister Jean found a small apartment for us one floor above her apartment. Danforth Avenue was an area of small shops. Dress stores, shoe stores, accessories, camera….. all sorts of small stores, our big stores were all downtown. All of the buildings were three story and most of them had a store on the ground level and rented the other two floors as apartments. So we started out in what was called a Batchelor apartment, tiny kitchen and bathroom and medium sized bedroom/living room. It was really small, but it was all ours.

Transportation was at the door as the tram service was excellent and connected to a bus service all over the city.

It took a while for me to get used to the food, it all tasted so different whether it was morning cereal or meat. I ate mostly boiled eggs for the first month as they tasted "Scottish". Money was another difficulty as I needed help translating pounds, shilling and pence to dollars. My first trip to the supermarket with Jean was quite an adventure as I kept asking her every ten minutes "how much have I spent now?" and she had to translate this into British currency.

It took some time to be comfortable with my peers at work. They knew nothing of Scotland and all things Canadian were new to me. They were really nice but didn't converse much with me. First, they didn't know what to say, and of course, the Scottish accent was confusing as was much of our terminology. Case in point, most working folks in Scotland didn't have an alarm clock and some who did had trouble getting up in the cold mornings. We had usually had one person in a tenement, you know the type, who seemed to have a built-in alarm clock and wakened early. In the jute mills, where most people worked, the gates were closed just after starting time, so if you were late you didn't work that day. So they hired this person for about a shilling a week and he would go round and knock on your door and called out "y'up" until you answered "m'up". This process was called appropriately "being knocked-up in the morning". First morning I was late for work I mentioned that I needed someone to "knock me up" there was silence and shock on the faces of my workmates. Of course, they were too polite to say anything and it took a while for me to be careful about what I said, although I didn't know what was wrong. There were many words and expressions that were quite innocent in Scotland and meant something entirely different in Canada. Of course, we could laugh about it later but, in the beginning, my workmates didn't know what to make of this sweet little foul mouthed foreigner.

The girls were excited about The Avon Lady visiting the office. I had no idea what they were talking about. I just tagged along to the lunch and coffee breaks like the tail on the donkey and slowly learned what was important to Canadians. The girls were so excited about TV, quite new in Canada and not known in Scotland. Sid Ceasar and "Your Show of Shows" was re-hashed continually in conversation, again I had no idea and didn't want to show my ignorance by asking.

Eventually we adapted and purchased our own TV and Yes! I was as excited as everyone else about Sid Ceasar and Imogene Coca although a lot of the humour was lost on me. We also bought a small table for our TV and a bed-settee and some comfy chairs. We didn't have the money for a kitchen table but were saving for it. Our savings took a tumble when Norman, without my knowing, came home one day with a new Accordion and announced he had signed up for lessons. WHY? I was upset – the first of many times. I was so homesick. We eventually got our kitchen table but it always bothered me that the Accordion came first.

Norman immediately found friends as a drummer in a Toronto Pipe Band. Who wouldn't want his talents? A lead drummer direct from Scotland and a World Class Scottish Pipe Band.....he now had about forty buddies and they had weekly rehearsals, parades, competitions (many out of town) and many social occasions.

I joined the Congregational Church on Danforth Avenue where I could walk to church and weekly rehearsals for their choir. Norman was not interested in church. I went alone.

First choir rehearsal went well. In those days good church music was known whether you were in Germany, Scotland or Canada as many of the world's great composers were also church musicians and their music was known worldwide. Many of the anthems I already knew------if I closed my eyes I was back in my wee Kirk in Scotland.

As I went to don my robe for my first church service I followed other members into the robing room. One of the women pulled me back "Don't go in there Anna, that is the men's robing room" "Strange" I thought, as we all used the same room in Scotland. I found the reason as I walked into the other room to find everyone in their slips or petticoats. This was Canada in September, temperature 90 degrees with about 80 percent humidity and no air conditioning in church. You generate heat from singing, the   choir robes were heavy and retained the heat so it made sense to wear as little as possible. Still, it was very strange to me, and I felt uncomfortable as I thought that everyone in the congregation knew I was in my underwear.

We had arrived in Toronto at the end of August and I was an employee of Pitney-Bowes by the second week in September .... The heat was really a problem. There was no air conditioning in the office, this was 1954, and the rule was that when the indoor temperature reached 90 degrees we were allowed to go home. On those days Norman would also be home and we would drive with Jean and her husband Bill to a lake Simcoe North of Toronto and find relief at one of the small resorts that had protected lake swimming, getting back home about ten or eleven at night (thank goodness Jean lived just downstairs). The cool didn't last for long by the time we were half way home (no air conditioned car) we were hot and perspiring again. Unfortunately, the nights were not much cooler than the days. This was a trial after the coolness of a Scottish summer.

Then, less than two months after we arrived, Toronto was hit by a hurricane ....HAZEL. Starting in the Caribbean about October 5th 1954 where it was first classified as a hurricane, it ravaged the east coast of U.S.A. before seeming to dissipate. Hazel began to lose power. However, it reached The Great Lakes and began to gather momentum as it moved over water. Toronto, which had expected to be the end of a depleting storm ended up on October 16th with seventy mile an hour winds and torrential rains. This would not have been the tragedy it turned out to be but there had been steady, heavy rain for about two weeks prior, the ground was fully saturated and the storm rain was run-off which went directly into the rivers and waterways causing flooding and roaring rivers.

There were 81 deaths, mostly in an area that had been re-claimed from the Humber river and built into a residential neighborhood. In the onslaught of wind and rain the river burst its banks and re-claimed its original path , tearing houses from their foundations and carrying them with their occupants down into Lake Ontario. The river was so wild that rescue boats could not be sent out and our first responders stood by helplessly as many were carried to their deaths.

We were safe in our location, just heavy winds and rain but, gosh, we got those in Scotland. However, we got a frantic telegram next day from Mum "Saw the headlines STOP we are so worried STOP Let us know at once you are safe STOP" With no telephone, and letters taking 5 days each way by boat a telegram though expensive was the fastest means of communication. We sent off a telegram right away re-assuring them and then sent off a letter with particulars. But it brought home the fact that we were so far apart.

CHRISTMAS VISIT HOME

23

I was homesick that first year in Toronto and it was decided that I should go home at Christmas for two weeks. I was to go alone as we didn't have money for two air fares.

I had never been on an airplane before - we are talking 1955 and they were the old propeller planes, it was kind of scary. But I was used to being alone.

Norman had been lead drummer in a Dundee Scottish Pipe Band and had joined a Highland Band just after we arrived in Canada. He was an excellent lead drummer and soon had many buddies who played traditional Scottish Pipe music. They had weekly rehearsals, many club activities, and performed on many occasions in Toronto and the surrounding areas.

As I arrived at the airport on the day of my flight I was held back as the others boarded. I thought it was because of my immigration status. Boarding a flight was different then. Passengers were escorted out of the terminal building, across the airstrip to our waiting plane where we climbed the steps to get on board.

I was finally cleared after everyone else had boarded and was surprised by two lines of pipers in full Highland regalia who piped me over the tarmac and played as I mounted the steps to the plane. Passengers all agog at the windows as they took in the scene.

Finally got to my seat as a nice older lady by the window greeted me with "So much noise for a tiny person like you? So you are what all the fuss is about?" She said this in a kind manner, and when she found out that this was my first flight she graciously gave up her window seat to me.

Our flight took off on a gray December day thru' thick clouds. I forgot to be afraid as I watched the airport and the people become a world in miniature. Suddenly.....WE WERE IN BRIGHT SUNSHINE. As we rose above the magnificent, white fluffy clouds, they looked so friendly and inviting I thought they would be so lovely to walk on.

I don't remember meals on board but I do remember that all our flight attendants were male (this was transatlantic flight circa 1955). Young, strong and very responsible, you just knew that in an emergency they would take care of everything.

We landed in New York, my seating companion left and was replaced by a young woman whose destination was Glasgow. She was a first time flyer and also a movie buff - couldn't wait to inform me of a movie she had just seen and a phrase she couldn't shake "point of no return". As she explained to me "It's a certain part of a flight over the ocean when the plane can neither go back or move forward to safety in an emergency". I don't know if that was true or not but she certainly believed it.

With a very long flight ahead, stewards brought pillows and blankets. I was tired and was soon sound asleep. For how long I didn't know, when I felt a hand shaking my arm. I opened my eyes as my seat partner said in an excited voice "We're here" "Scotland so soon" I said. "No" she replied in hushed tones "The point of no return".

However we did arrive safely and I got an airport bus to take me to the train station where I waited for a train to Dundee. Luckily, I just had one suitcase and a young man came to my aid and saw me safely on board.

As we reached the station in Dundee Dad was waiting for me and had a taxi waiting to take me home. I was so happy to be once again with family. Both my sisters were married and had children. Betty had two bairns and Margaret had three, just wee people, the eldest being just three years old.

For the first few days I visited all the grandparents, uncles, aunts and cousins. Christmas was about nine days away with the excitement and joy that it always brings. First Saturday at home I had a wonderful evening in town with both sisters and their husbands. Very capable aunts took over the baby-sitting duties. Such a lovely night out.

Tragedy struck swiftly. Two days later Dad got a phone call. I was upstairs when I heard my Mum cry out "Oh! No! Dave!". she sounded frantic. I hurried downstairs and got the shocking and unexpected news. One of our wee ones had died suddenly. So much sorrow, it was just about unbearable. I don't know how we all got through the planning of the funeral. Family came by, but what could they do?

Most of us could not stop crying. Dad tried to comfort us and hold things together. He was so worried about Mum's health as her heart was not too strong. Dad was also the "go to" guy in every emergency, but this was overwhelming and he had to remain calm and steady while mourning so hard himself.

Priest came by the house for a small private service which took place a few days before Christmas.

Thru' all the sorrow it was the joy of Christmas that brought us back from grief and back to some semblance of order. Margaret and Betty had their other kids to think about and it was still Christmas. The children sensed something was wrong. Being such little children though, they lived in the moment, and they had the same excitement on Christmas morning as toddlers everywhere and the grown-ups did their best for the kids.

You would think that after such a tragedy we would have some time to recover, but life doesn't seem to be that way. A few days after Christmas, David, age fifteen, answered the door and came to get me. At the door was a policeman...my heart stopped! On being asked in (thankfully Mum was resting upstairs) he told me that Dad had been in a serious accident and he was here to take me to the hospital. I was eldest of the family and Mum was incapacitated so I had to see to hospital procedures. Dad had been so hurt and preoccupied with what had happened to his family that a car had hit him while he was crossing the street. He was seriously injured and had a forty percent chance of surviving. I signed the necessary papers and got to see Dad but he was not aware of me.

At home I tried to explain to Mum that Dad was in hospital but kept details to a minimum. Strict visiting rules were in place in Scottish hospitals in the 1950s and the rules could be broken only under the most extreme of circumstances. So I was at home trying to keep Mum calm.

We had no phone at home, usual for Scots households at that time. For the first three days I walked every few hours during the day to the phone booth on the corner. Money in slot, dial hospital and hold my breath as "sister" answered my enquiry. Always there was no change.

Standing in the phone booth on the fourth morning and filled with apprehension I prayed to my God "I know all life and death are in your hands, dear Lord, and I trust you in all things but please don't take him now". The prayer did nothing to calm me as I started to dial. Then I heard the words in my head "Don't be a doubting Thomas". The nurse answered my question with "There has been no change"

Now I had to give the bleak news to Mum (I remember it now almost sixty years later as if it had just happened). As Mum looked at me anxiously and I was about to tell her the news.....Suddenly, the whole room was filled with a luminous mist that seemed that it was glowing with a beautiful light which was also warm and calming. No one else was aware of it and there seemed to be no time to it AND I KNEW!!!!!! Mum said to me "What is it? Anna, you are smiling" Mum thought the worry had got the best of me. I answered "Dad is going to be all right" As I walked to the phone that afternoon the calm feeling stayed with me. Upon phoning, I got the answer I had been praying for "He seems to have turned the corner and there is good hope for a recovery".

I never told anyone about this until I was in my seventies and trying to help a sick friend yet it was and is the most real happening of my life.

In a few days Dad was conscious, Mother and I were allowed to visit and Dad got better every day. He was still very ill and still in hospital one week later.

In Toronto I still had work and a husband to take care of. Business had given me some extra time-off due to the circumstances but that was all the time they could give me. So the day of my flight came. Saying goodbye to Dad in hospital and a very shaken, upset Mother was so difficult but by now my sisters were taking over.

Such a long flight home with so many sad memories and worries for Mom, Dad and family. Norman met me at the airport, I had phoned him all the details and he knew how difficult my trip had been. I felt safe now to give in to all my emotions and cried most of the way home.

At the apartment Norman had placed our most comfortable armchair in front of the TV with a box of chocolates and TV guide on the side table. Home at last, away from the turmoil and heart breaking sadness.

We had our "tea" and half an hour later Norman reached for his coat. "I have to go Hon, the band is playing tonight". The door closed and I was alone with my painful thoughts.

I remember when we had first landed in Canada and I quote my original thoughts. "Upon arriving in Canada (in Montreal, I think) my first memories were of standing on deck, unbearably hot after the cool of a Scottish summer. I was in a long queue of several hundred new emigrants waiting to go through immigration. I WAS ALONE. My husband of one year, though raised in Scotland had been born in Canada and had no need for immigration formalities. He was eager to view his new country and so I waited alone in the heat, among strangers. Was this a portend of things to come?"

Now it seemed prophetic in the most terrible way.

24

Five months after we arrived Norman's mum, Dad and sister emigrated so now their family was complete......where they had started. They brought me a gift from my family, a gold locket with pictures of Mum and Dad, it brought me to tears. I was glad for Norman but I so missed my ain folks.

About this time we bought a used car, a Ford Fairlane, I don't remember what the purchase cost us per month but it was nice to have our own car. Of course I didn't drive, this was the early fifties, so Norman had the car for work on week-days. As we worked in different parts of the town the street car was still my means of transportation, it was an easy commute from the door, a straight route to Bloor Street and a five minute walk from there to the office.

About this time I joined an Opera Company, it was made up mostly of Italians (there were many in our Cosmopolitan town) who not only sang in Italian but also spoke only in Italian. Most, like me, new immigrants looking for the familiarity of home. But this was not my Opera where most of our composers were English and where we also did light opera, Belle of New York and Rose Marie, Gilbert and Sullivan. I did become friends with a Canadian girl but she lived at the other end of Toronto. Like me, didn't drive a car and, as Norman and I had no phone, we had no means of communicating. The opera we were rehearsing was " La Traviatta ", to be learned in Italian. I stayed until the performances and then left. Why would I even think that this would be like my Dundee Opera?????

Norman's two friends since first grade decided to emigrate and arrived in Canada in the Summer of 1955. They came to Toronto as Norman was already settled there. We were no longer a couple but a foursome. First off they rented an apartment nearby then started looking for work. Of course, Norman drove them wherever they needed to go. Andy was engaged to a Dundee girl, with plans for her to come over in the next year, Bill was the quiet, shy type who always just felt comfortable around his buddies. Having no TV, they would join us in the evenings and not being handy in the kitchen (typical) "Come early and have y'er tea with us" said Norman. O.K. So most evenings and on the week-ends they were with us….just like family…but not my family.

They helped pay for some groceries (but no help with the cooking, typical). They also thanked us sometimes with a restaurant dinner. Always the four of us, I shouldn't complain, they were nice guys and we had some great times together. They picked up where they left off in Scotland as the three of them would go to soccer games, play billiards and the boys would go with Norman to Pipe Band practice. And Norman did not have to leave me alone when , say, he was out of town with the band. The boys would take me to the beach or the movies. I remember one trip to Stratford-on-Avon for a Shakespeare play I wanted to see. Andy, by this time, could drive. The boys had no liking for Shakespeare but we had a great day. Bill, Andy and I. Norman was doing a parade somewhere.

I was doing my own thing too! I had belonged to the Royal Scottish Dance Society back home and joined a branch of it in Toronto. It was great doing the old Scottish dances and I made some girlfriends. Not asked to dance too often though... there were strict rules in society in those days, and most of the single boys were very wary of a young woman with a wedding band on her left hand.

I had been searching for a vocal studio so that I could continue my musical studies. Finally found a good vocal coach in Mrs Morrison. Her studio, I was told, was in the former home of the Lieutenant Governor of Ontario, it was a beautiful mansion which had been converted to accommodate musicians of all sorts. Piano, violin, voice, practice rooms. Teachers in all the performing arts .

Mrs Morrison's studio was a large, ground floor room with a grand balcony overlooking High Park. It had high ceilings, walnut wall paneling, great acoustics and, of course, a grand piano. She was a good coach, I learned much from her, and, with her many connections, I got quite a few concert appearances and church work.

When taking private lessons you really don't have connections with students other than those with lessons before and after yours, and it was just "hello" as teacher was starting her next lesson. There were about forty students at the studio. However, our studio had a special recital once a month which was a unique experience. An excellent accompanist was hired from Toronto School of Music and the concert was for a few hours on a Saturday afternoon. Of course, all her students, apart from the techniques of the voice and stage deportment, were also working on special music for themselves.

Our teacher would chose about eight students working on various Oratorios, Opera, art numbers, even some modern music (when you are classically trained you can sing any kind of music). The audience was strictly for her students and we critiqued each number and could offer our advice to the soloists. Observing others, you can hear and see more clearly when things are right, even more so when things are not right. It was a great learning experience and the audience students were very supportive of the soloists.

I had been working for a few months on a coloratura aria "Juliet's Waltz Song" from Romeo and Juliet by Gounod and I was asked to try it out at one of our student recitals. That Saturday arrived and I stood in front of my peers. I had a wonderful accompanist who seemed to be one with me and the music.....perfect support.

How can I explain this? Sometimes, for a singer, everything seems to come together...the breath control, the relaxation, the tone placement, the agility. Without effort it seems that the voice and the music are one and you can just feel the emotion of the song. It is a euphoric experience when you truly know "the joy of singing". It is a wonderful feeling. My peers gave me raucous approval and I even got a 'well done" from Mrs Morrison. This had been a difficult coloratura aria and I felt that I had done well (all singers are their own strictest critics).

Going home on the streetcar this feeling stayed with me 'til I got home. Upon opening the door to our living room (we had moved to a larger apartment) there were Norman, Andy and Bill playing cards, drinking beer, the room smoky from their cigarettes. Couldn't wait to tell Norman how well I had done. "Good for you hon," he said I'm glad you are pleased with yourself" "Bill, what was the last card you played?"

I thought "what's wrong with this picture?" I was not part of a marriage as Bill, Andy and Norman were a threesome, all good school pals. It seemed that I was the outsider.

Norman was not a bad person. He was just being a typical Scottish guy. Most of them, after marrying got back to normal. And he did the "guy" things with his pals again. The wife, after the first year, in most cases would have, or be with child (this was the early fifties), was surrounded by supportive family, doing "the girl thing". Visiting with grandmas, aunts, shopping for baby things with Mum, going to the movies with sisters and their kids. It was the usual progression of a marriage in those days.

I was as strong and resilient as other Scottish women, but, in Canada, I was lost in this new situation . Norman thought everything was normal…. but I was becoming an island without my loving family. The talents which I thought brought us together seemed now to pull us apart. Norman had no interest in my singing and Pipe Band was just another "guy thing".

We had now been married just over three years when I began to feel that our marriage was going nowhere. The boys vacationed with us and even came to dinner on our Anniversary. We didn't discuss our problems….what was the point? Norman had his friends, his wife, his family, his Pipe Band...for him life was just great......for me.......NOT SO MUCH....But there was no use complaining. These were the fifties and marriage was for keeps.

However, it was my Birthday in 1957 that crystallized my knowledge that this marriage was over. Pipe Band was on a week-end trip to Buffalo, New York. Andy and Bill had gone along on the trip..

Saturday afternoon about three-o-clock, the phone rings. It is Arthur, one of the young men who ran the Scots Country dancing. "I just called to wish you a Happy Birthday" he said. "Norman and you going out to celebrate?" "No", I said "Norm is away with the Band, I am by myself" "We can't have that on your birthday" said Arthur "How about I take you to dinner and a movie to celebrate?" Arthur was about five years older than me, single, and I knew that he really liked me and he was always a gentleman.....I thought we were good friends.

I met Arthur at the subway station, we had a lovely dinner, saw a movie, then Arthur brought me back to the subway station and saw me on the bus for home. It was a nice friendly evening, but, during dinner I was thinking "this is not the way it should be" I realized that there was no way to stay in a marriage that didn't exist. Finally, I realized how ridiculous this was and how vulnerable I was because I was so lonely.

Next morning (Sunday) I approached a retired couple I knew at church. They had a small house on the edge of town and had been telling me that their renter had just left. They rented out a small furnished bedroom, so I was able to rent bed and board with them. I could have breakfast and dinner on week-days when I was working and full meals on week-ends. It would do for a start until I figured out just what I should do. Should I stay in Toronto, where I had a nice career and had lived for the past three years? Or should I go home to Scotland? Either way I could not move forward with my life, I was still a married woman and divorce was unthinkable in those days. There was no returning to Norman, the marriage was over.

Work at Pitney-Bowes was going well. After about six months I was moved to Accounts Receivable Department, I loved the work, was good at it and after about six months when I was well acquainted with the department was asked to be assistant to the Supervisor. And a year later, when he left the firm I was asked to take over as Supervisor. I was now making (for a woman in those days) a very nice salary and could well afford to make it on my own.

When Norman returned home on Sunday night I told him I would be leaving at the end of the week. He couldn't believe it........I told him I wanted the free time so I could pursue my music further. It was not the truth as I just wanted out...but it was easier to use my singing as an excuse. I think Norman had the idea that I would try this and, when it didn't work out, I would return. No one could believe I would leave "Norman is such a great guy" they said. Sure, he was so busy being a "great guy", he forgot to be a good husband.

I told Norman I would leave on Friday night after work and asked him not to be home. It worked out well as he had a Pipe Band parade. Reg , my retired friend from church helped me move. Going to a furnished bedroom I took only my clothes, music, personal items, my little record player and a few records. I had been employed thru' the almost four years of our marriage and contributed all my wages to building our home but I left everything......furniture, car, crystal and fine china and linens from our wedding. I had no need for them and I just wanted out. Thinking back on it, Norman didn't offer to move in with his buddies and let me stay in the apartment, the funny thing is that I didn't expect him to.

Making a good wage at Pitney-Bowes and my only expenses being rent, music lessons and lunches and a few fundamentals, I started fresh with my first pay check.

25

It took me quite some time to adjust to my new living arrangements. I had been used to running my own home, and was so independent. Reg and Evelyn were a nice old couple and did their best to be kind and share their home with me. I was still alone but it was of my own choosing. The worst feeling is to be alone in a crowd...or a marriage.

I did not share any of this with my family as they would just worry... and what could they do? As working folks we did not have the luxury of a home phone so I could not talk to my sisters, and to discuss such a life changing situation in letters was impossible.........letters in those days took five days each way which would have made for quite a stilted conversation. I would have to figure this out for myself.

When a marriage fails you wonder what went wrong and what could you have done to save it. There is always a feeling of guilt and you lose confidence in yourself.

Thank goodness for music. It never let me down, singing is my comfort when I am sad and my joy when I am happy.......in all things music is my anchor. Since a child music has always been my touchstone and always lets me express my emotions.

My Dad always used to say "it's an ill wind that doesn't blow somebody some good". In the gale that I was in I turned to my music and that was the saving of me. Mrs Morrison, God bless her, knew what was going on, she kept introducing new and interesting challenges and got me solos in more churches in town. Evelyn, my new landlady , turned out to be quite a good pianist and she and I would work on new numbers in the evenings.

Of course, I was still at Pitney-Bowes which kept me busy and connected with all the social activities in a large office...... Birthdays, Weddings, an occasional Baby Shower, even "The Avon Lady" was a diversion. After about three months I began to settle into my new way of living. Still didn't know what I should do. I had now been in Canada a little over three years. To pack up and go home meant to me that I had failed.

I loved my job and was doing well. I had a few girl friends I could socialize with. Dating was out of the question whether in Canada or Scotland.....I was still a married woman. Anyway, I had enough of "guys" to last me for a lifetime.

One day I went to my lesson to find Mrs Morrison all excited, unusual for her, she was usually so calm and competent. She told me " I have a new singer, a wonderful tenor who has done much professional work in town and did have his own radio show, his name is Tommy Hender" I didn't get to meet this singer as his lessons did not coincide with mine. I did hear much about him though from my teacher, as did most of my fellow singers. "Tommy Hender never has a bad lesson, Tommy Hender's diction is perfect, Tommy Hender's top notes are never strained they are beautifully placed," and on coming in straight from work one day with my music in disarray " Tommy Hender always knows what he is doing and always has all his music in order" Tommy Hender was disliked before we even met him, poor guy.

One day, everything seemed to go just right and I had a really good lesson. My vocal coach was so pleased " if you keep this up Anna, I might let you sing a duet with Tommy Hender" Huh! I thought, I wouldn't sing a duet with Tommy Hender if he was the last tenor on earth..........Little did I know.

My life at this point was an emptiness . They say nature abhors a vacuum and I guess had other plans for me..........it would lead me to a new life in a new country.

Made in the USA
Charleston, SC
11 December 2013